Revised and Updated Edition

FINANCING SECRETS
of a
MILLIONAIRE REAL ESTATE INVESTOR

D0795713

Revised and Updated Edition

FINANCING SECRETS

of a

MILLIONAIRE REAL ESTATE INVESTOR

William Bronchick, Esq.

with Gary Licata

PUBLISHING

New York

This publication is designed to provide accurate and authoritative information in regard to the subject matter covered. It is sold with the understanding that the publisher is not engaged in rendering legal, accounting, or other professional service. If legal advice or other expert assistance is required, the services of a competent professional person should be sought.

Editorial Director: Jennifer Farthing
Development Editor: Joshua Martino
Production Editor: Julio Espin
Typesetting: International Typesetting and Composition
Cover Design: Rod Hernandez

© 2007 by William Bronchick

Published by Kaplan Publishing
A Division of Kaplan Inc.

All rights reserved. The text of this publication, or any part thereof, may not be reproduced in any manner whatsoever without written permission from the publisher.

Printed in the United States of America

May 2007
07 08 09 10 9 8 7 6 5 4 3 2 1

ISBN 10: 1-4277-5462-4
ISBN 13: 978-1-4277-5462-2

Kaplan Publishing books are available at special quantity discounts to use for sales promotions, employee premiums, or educational purposes. Please email our Special Sales Department to order or for more information at kaplanpublishing@kaplan.com, or write to Kaplan Publishing, 888 7th Avenue, 22nd Floor, New York, NY 10106.

CONTENTS

CHAPTER 1

Introduction to Real Estate Financing

Knowledge is power.

—Francis Bacon

Financing has traditionally been, and will always be, an integral part of the purchase and sale of real estate. Few people have the funds to purchase properties for all cash, and those that do rarely sink all of their money in one place. Even institutional and corporate buyers of real estate use borrowed money to buy real estate.

This book explains how to utilize real estate financing in the most effective and profitable way possible. Mostly, this book focuses on acquisition techniques for investors, but these techniques are also applicable to potential homeowners.

Understanding the Time Value of Money

In order to understand real estate financing, it is important that you understand the time value of money. Because of inflation, a dollar today is generally worth less in the future. Thus, while real estate values may increase, an all-cash purchase may not be economically feasible, because the investor's cash may be utilized in more effective ways.

The cost of borrowing money is expressed in interest payments, usually a percent of the loan amount. Interest payments can be calculated in a variety of ways, the most common of which is simple interest. Simple interest is calculated by multiplying the loan amount by the interest rate, then dividing it up into periods, (12 months, 15 years, etc.).

> ☛ **Example:** A $100,000 loan at 12% simple interest is $12,000 per year, or $1,000 per month. To calculate monthly simple-interest payments, take the loan amount (principal), multiply it by the interest rate, and then divide by 12. In this example, $100,000 × .12 = $12,000 per year ÷ 12 = $1,000 per month.

Mortgage loans are generally not paid in simple interest but rather by amortization schedules (discussed in Chapter 4), calculated by amortization tables (see Appendix A). *Amortization,* derived from the Latin word "amorta" (death), is to pay down or "kill" a debt. Amortized payments remain the same throughout the life of the loan but are broken down into interest and principal. The payments made near the beginning of the loan are mostly interest, while the payments near the end are mostly principal. Lenders increase their return and reduce their risk by having most of the profit (interest) built into the front of the loan.

The Concept of Leverage

Leverage is the process of using borrowed money to make a return on an investment. Let's say you bought a house using all of your cash for $100,000. If the property were to increase in value 10 percent over 12 months, it would now be worth $110,000. Your return on investment would be 10 percent annually (of course, you would actually net less because you would incur costs in selling the property).

Equity = Property value – Mortgage debt

The Federal Reserve and Interest Rates

The Federal Reserve (the Fed) is an independent entity created by an Act of Congress in 1913 to serve as the central bank of the United States (www.federalreserve.gov). There are 12 regional banks that make up the Federal Reserve System. While the regional banks are corporations whose stock is owned by member banks, the shareholders have no influence over the Federal Reserve banks' policies.

Among other things, the function of the Fed is to try to regulate inflation and credit conditions in the U.S. economy. The Federal Reserve banks also supervise and regulate depository institutions.

So how does the Fed's policy affect interest rates on loans? To put it simply, by manipulating "supply and demand." The Fed changes the money supply by increasing or decreasing reserves in the banking system through the buying and selling of securities. The changes in the money supply, in turn, affect interest rates: the lower the supply of money, the higher the interest rate that is charged for loans between banks. The more it costs a bank to borrow money, the more they charge in interest to consumers to borrow that money. The preceding is a simplified explanation, because there are other factors in the world economy that affect interest rates and money supply. And, of course, there are also widely varying opinions by economists as to what factors drive the economy and interest rates. In the last few years, mortgage interest rates have been influenced by factors other than the Federal Reserve rate, such as the supply of foreign capital from Asia into the United States.

If you purchased a property using $10,000 of your own cash and $90,000 in borrowed money, a 10 percent increase in value would still result in $10,000 of increased equity, but your return on cash is 100 percent ($10,000 investment yielding $20,000 in equity). Of course, the borrowed money isn't free; you would have to incur loan costs and interest payments in borrowing money. However, by renting the property in the meantime, you would offset the interest expense of the loan.

Calculating Return on Investment

Annual return on investment (ROI) is the interest rate you yield on your cash investment. It is calculated by taking the annual cash flow and/or equity increase and dividing it by the amount of cash invested. Return on investment includes the equity increase, whereas "cash-on-cash" is simply cash invested divided by annual cash flow. The cash-on-cash formula is affected by your operating expenses on the property, as well as payments you make for interest on your loan, which in turn affect your cash flow.

Let's also look at the income versus expense ratios. If you purchased a property using all cash for $100,000 and collected $1,000 per month in rent, your annual cash-on-cash return is 12 percent (simply divide the annual income, $12,000, by the amount of cash invested, $100,000).

If you borrowed $90,000 and the payments on the loan were $660 per month, your annual net income is $4,080 ($12,000 – [$660 × 12]), but your annual cash-on-cash return is about 40 percent (annual cash of $4,080 divided by $10,000 invested).

So, if you purchased ten properties with 10 percent down and 90 percent financing, you could increase your overall profit by more than threefold. Of course, you would also increase your risk, which will be discussed in more detail in Chapter 4.

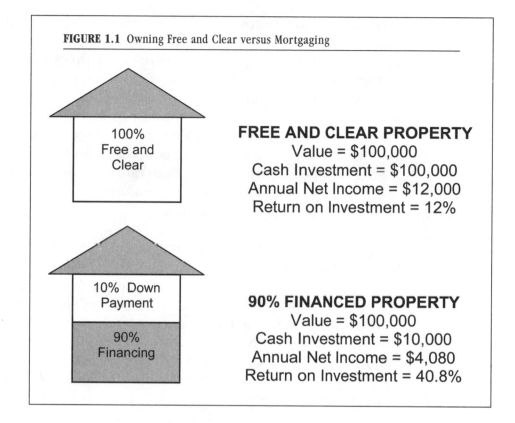

FIGURE 1.1 Owning Free and Clear versus Mortgaging

100%
Free and
Clear

FREE AND CLEAR PROPERTY
Value = $100,000
Cash Investment = $100,000
Annual Net Income = $12,000
Return on Investment = 12%

10% Down
Payment

90%
Financing

90% FINANCED PROPERTY
Value = $100,000
Cash Investment = $10,000
Annual Net Income = $4,080
Return on Investment = 40.8%

Owning Property "Free and Clear"

For some investors, the goal is to own properties "free and clear," that is, with no mortgage debt. While this is a worthy goal, it does not necessarily make financial sense. See Figure 1.1.

☛ **Example:** Consider a $100,000 property that brings in $10,000 per year in net income (*net* means gross rents collected, less expenses, such as property taxes, maintenance, utilities, and hazard insurance). The $100,000 in equity thus yields a 10 percent annual return on investment ($10,000, the annual net cash flow, divided by $100,000, the equity investment). This formula is the property's capitalization or "cap" rate, which has nothing to do with the mortgage payments for the property or the amount of cash you have invested. The reason investors use cap rate is to compare potential return on investment with other investments, without regard to the financing on the property. However, cap rate alone is not necessarily the only factor to consider. For example, if one property has a cap rate of 7% and another property has a 11% cap rate it would seem obvious that the higher cap rate would be desirable. This is not necessarily so because with a higher cap rate can come higher risk. You must determine if you are comfortable with higher risk associated with higher cap rate.

If the property were financed for 80 percent of its value ($80,000) at 7.5 percent interest, the monthly payment would be approximately $560 per month, or $6,720 per year. Net rent of $10,000 per year minus $6,720 in debt payments equals $3,280 per year in net cash flow. Divide the $3,280 in annual cash flow by the $20,000 in equity and you have a 16.4 percent return on investment. Furthermore, with $80,000 more cash, you could buy four more properties. As you can see, financing, even when you don't necessarily "need" to do so, can be more profitable than investing all of your cash in one property.

How Financing Affects the Real Estate Market

Because financing plays a large part in real estate sales, it also affects values; the higher the interest rate, the larger your monthly payment. Conversely, the lower the interest rate, the lower the monthly payment. Thus, the lower the interest rate, the larger the mortgage loan you can afford to pay. Consequently, the larger the mortgage you can afford, the more the seller can ask for in the sales prices.

Also, people with less cash are usually more concerned with their payment than the total amount of the purchase price or loan amount. On the other hand, people with all cash are more concerned with price. Because most buyers borrow most of the purchase price, the prices of houses are affected by financing. Thus, when interest rates are low, housing prices tend to increase, because people can afford a higher monthly payment. Conversely, when interest rates are higher, people cannot afford as much a payment, generally driving real estate prices down.

Since the mid-1990s, the prices of real estate have dramatically increased in most parts of the country. The American economy has grown, the job growth during this period has been good, but most important, interest rates have been low. In some parts of the country, local real estate markets have softened, but escaped a major bust because of low interest rates.

How Financing Affects Particular Transactions

When valuing residential properties, real estate appraisers generally follow a series of standards set forth by professional associations (the most well known is the Appraisal Institute). Sales of comparable properties are the general benchmark for value. Appraisers look not just at housing sale prices of comparable houses, but also at the financing associated with the sales of these houses. If the house was owner-financed (discussed in Chapter 9), the interest rate is generally higher than conventional rates and/or the price is inflated. The price is generally inflated because the seller's credit qualifications are looser than that of a bank, which means the buyer will not generally complain about the price.

Take a Cue from Other Industries

The explosion of the electronics market, the automobile market, and other large-ticket purchase markets is directly affected by financing. Just thumb through the Sunday newspapers and you will see headlines such as "no money down" or "no payments for one year." These retailers have learned that financing moves a product because it makes it easier for people to justify the purchase. Likewise, the price of a house may be stretched a bit more when it translates to just a few dollars more per month in mortgage payments.

Appraisals on income properties are done in a variety of ways, one of which is the "income" approach. The *income approach* looks at the value of the property versus the rents the property can produce. While financing does not technically come into the equation, it does affect the property's profitability to the investor. Thus, a property that can be financed at a lower interest rate will be more attractive to the investor if cash flow is a major concern. The income approach is not generally used by appraisers for properties of four units or less.

Tax Impact of Financing

Down payments made on a property as an investor are not tax-deductible. In fact, a large down payment offers no tax advantage at all because the investor's tax basis is based on the purchase price, not the amount he or she puts down. However, because mortgage interest is a deductible expense, the investor does better tax wise by saving his or her cash. Think about it: the higher the monthly mortgage payment, the less cash flow, the less taxable income each year. While positive cash flow is desirable, it does not necessarily mean that a property is more profitable because it has more cash flow. A larger down payment will obviously increase monthly cash flow, but it is not always the best use of your money.

How Real Estate Investors Use Financing

As discussed above, investors use mortgage loans to increase their leverage. The more money an investor can borrow, the more he or she can leverage the investment. Rarely do investors use all cash to purchase properties, and when they do, it is on a short-term basis. They usually refinance the property to get their cash back or sell the property for cash.

The challenge is that loans for investors are treated as high-risk by lenders when compared to noninvestor (owner-occupied properties) loans. Lenders often look at leveraged investments as risky and are less willing to loan money to investors. Lenders assume (often correctly) that the less of your own money you have invested, the more likely you will be to walk away from a bad property. In addition, fewer investor loan programs mean less competition in the industry, which leads to higher loan costs for the investor. The goal of the investor thus is to put forth as little cash as possible, pay the least amount in loan costs and interest, while keeping personal risk at a minimum. This is quite a challenge, and this book will reveal some of the secrets for accomplishing this task.

When Is Cash Better Than Financing?

Using all cash to purchase a property may be better than financing in two particular situations. The first situation is a short-term deal, that is, you intend to sell the house shortly after you buy it (known as "flipping"). When you have the cash to close quickly, you can generally get a tremendous discount on the price of a house. In this case, financing may delay the transaction long enough to lose an opportunity. Cash also allows you to purchase properties at a larger discount. You've heard the expression, "money talks, BS walks." This is particularly true when making an offer to purchase a property through a real estate agent. The real estate agent is more likely to recommend to his or her client a purchase offer that is not contingent on the buyer obtaining bank financing.

> **Understanding a Cash Offer versus Paying All Cash**
>
> If you make a "cash offer" on a property, it does not necessarily mean you are using all of your own cash. It means the seller is receiving all cash, as opposed to the seller financing some part of the purchase price (discussed more fully in Chapter 9). Thus, you can borrow 100% of the purchase price from a lender and it will still be considered a "cash offer" if the seller gets all of his price at closing.

The second case is one in which you can use your retirement account. You can use the cash in your IRA or SEP to purchase real estate, and the income from the property is tax-deferred. In order to do this, you need an aggressive self-directed IRA custodian (oddly enough, most IRA custodians view real estate as "risky" and the stock market as "safe"). Two such custodians are Equity Trust, <www.trustetc. com>, or Entrust Administration, <http://www.theentrustgroup.com/>.

What to Expect from This Book

This book will show you how to finance properties with as little cash as possible, while maintaining minimum risk and maximum profit.

The first few chapters describe the mortgage loan process, legal details, and the banking industry. Chapter 4 covers different types of lenders and loans, and the benefits of each. Chapter 5 covers how to creatively use institutional loan programs as an investor. Chapters 6, 7, 8, and 9 cover creative, noninstitutional financing.

As with any technique on real estate acquisition or finance, you should review the process with a local professional, including an attorney. Also, keep in mind that while most of these ideas are applicable nationwide, local practices, laws, rules, customs, and market conditions may require variations or adaptations for your particular use.

Key Points

- Interest rates affect property values.
- Financing affects the value of a property to an investor.
- Investors use financing to leverage their investments.

A Legal Primer on Real Estate Loans

If there were no bad people there would be no good lawyers.

—Charles Dickens

Before we discuss lenders, loans, and loan terms, it is essential that you understand the legal fundamentals and paperwork involved with mortgage loans. By analogy, you cannot make a living buying and selling automobiles without a working knowledge of engines and car titles. Likewise, you need to understand how the paperwork fits into the real estate transaction. Without a working knowledge of the paperwork, you are at the mercy of those who have the knowledge. Furthermore, without the know-how your risk of a large mistake or missed opportunity increases tremendously.

What Is a Mortgage?

Most of us think of going to a bank to get a mortgage. Actually, you go to the bank to get a loan. Once you are approved for the loan, you sign a promissory note to the lender, which is a legal promise to pay. You also give the lender (not get) a mortgage as security for repayment of the note. A *mortgage* (also called a "deed of trust" in some states) is a security agreement under which the borrower pledges his or her property as collateral for payment. The mortgage document is recorded in the county property records, creating a lien on the property in favor of the lender. See Figure 2.1.

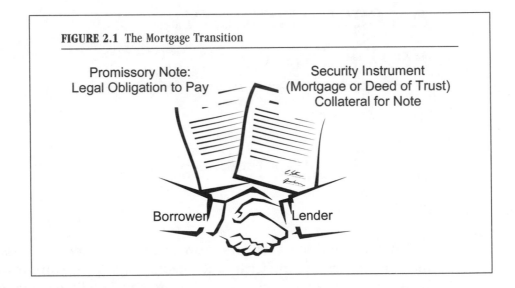

FIGURE 2.1 The Mortgage Transition

Promissory Note:
Legal Obligation to Pay

Security Instrument
(Mortgage or Deed of Trust)
Collateral for Note

Borrower   Lender

If the underlying obligation (the promissory note) is paid off, the lender must release the collateral (the mortgage). The release will remove the mortgage lien from the property. If you search the public records of a particular property, you will see many recorded mortgages that have been placed and released over the years.

Promissory Note in Detail

A note is an IOU or promise to pay; it is a legal obligation. A promissory note (also known as a "note" or "mortgage note") spells out the amount of the loan, the interest to be paid, how and when payments are made, and what happens if the borrower defaults. The note may also contain disclosures and other provisions required by federal or state law.

A Mortgage Note Is a Negotiable Instrument

Like a check, a mortgage note can be assigned and collected by whoever holds the note. As discussed in Chapter 3, mortgage notes are often bought, sold, traded, and hypothecated (pledged as collateral).

Most lenders use a form of note that is approved by the Federal National Mortgage Association (FNMA, or Fannie Mae). A sample form of this note can be found in Appendix C. The note is signed (in legal terms, "executed") by the borrower. The original note is held by the lender until the debt is paid in full, at which time the original note is returned to the borrower marked "paid in full."

A Promissory Note Is a Personal Obligation

Because promissory notes are personal obligations, the history of payments will appear on your credit file, even if the debt is used for investment. If you fail to pay on the note, your credit will be adversely affected, and you risk a lawsuit from the lender. Some notes are nonrecourse, that is, the lender cannot sue you personally. Although not always possible, you should try to make sure most of your debt is nonrecourse.

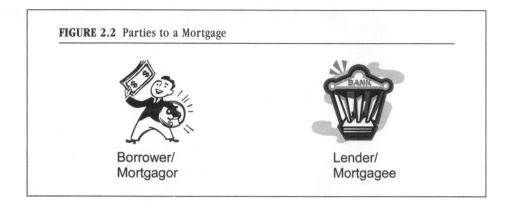

FIGURE 2.2 Parties to a Mortgage

Borrower/
Mortgagor

Lender/
Mortgagee

The Mortgage in Detail

The security agreement executed by the borrower pledges the property as collateral for the note. Known by most as a "mortgage," this document, when recorded (discussed below), creates a lien in favor of the lender. The mortgage agreement is generally a standardized form approved by FNMA. While the form of note is generally the same from state to state, the mortgage form differs slightly because the legal process of foreclosure (the lender's right to proceed against the collateral) is different in each state. See Figure 2.2.

The mortgage document will state that upon default of the note, the lender can exercise its right to foreclose on the property. Foreclosure is the process of lenders exercising their legal right to proceed against the collateral for the loan (discussed later in this chapter). It also places other obligations upon the borrower, such as

- maintaining the property,

- paying property taxes, and

- keeping the property insured.

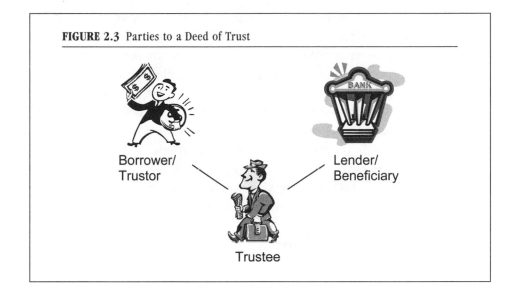

FIGURE 2.3 Parties to a Deed of Trust

Borrower/
Trustor

Lender/
Beneficiary

Trustee

The Deed of Trust

Some states (e.g., California) use a document called a "deed of trust" (a.k.a. "trust deed") rather than a mortgage. The *deed of trust* is a document in which the trustor (borrower) gives a deed to the neutral third party (trustee) to hold for the beneficiary (lender). A deed of trust is worded almost exactly the same as a mortgage, except for the names of the parties. Thus, the deed of trust and mortgage are essentially the same, other than the foreclosure process. See Figure 2.3.

The Public Recording System

The recording system gives constructive notice to the public of the transfer of an interest in property. Recording simply involves bringing the original document to the local county courthouse or county clerk's office. The original document is copied onto a computer file or onto microfiche and is returned to the new owner. There is a filing fee of about $6 to $10 per page for recording the document.

In addition, the county, city, and/or state may assess a transfer tax based on either the value of the property or the mortgage amount.

A deed or other conveyance does not have to be recorded to be a valid transfer of an interest. For example, what happens if John gives title to Mary, then he gives it again to Fred, and Fred records first? What happens if John gives a mortgage to ABC Savings and Loan, but the mortgage is not filed for six months, and then John immediately borrows from another lender who records its mortgage first? Who wins and loses in these scenarios?

Most states follow a "race-notice" rule, meaning that the first person to record his document, wins, so long as

- he received title in good faith,

- he paid value, and

- he had no notice of a prior transfer.

☞ **Example:** John buys a home and, in so doing, borrows $75,000 from ABC Savings Bank. John signs a promissory note and a mortgage pledging his home as collateral. Because ABC messes up the paperwork, the mortgage does not get recorded for 18 months. In the interim, John borrows $12,000 from The Money Store, for which he gives a mortgage as collateral. The Money Store records its mortgage, unaware of John's unrecorded first mortgage to ABC. The Money Store will now have a first mortgage on the property.

Priority of Liens

Most liens, like deeds, are "first in time, first in line." Thus, if a property is owned free and clear, a mortgage recorded will be a *first mortgage*. A mortgage recorded thereafter will be a *second mortgage* (sometimes called a *junior mortgage* because its lien position is behind the first mortgage). Likewise, any judgments or other liens recorded later are also junior liens. Holding a first mortgage is a desirable position because a foreclosure on a mortgage can wipe out all liens that are recorded behind it (called "junior lien holders"). The process of foreclosure will be discussed in more detail later in this chapter.

At the closing of a typical real estate sale, the seller conveys a deed to the buyer. Most buyers obtain a loan from a conventional lender for most of the cash needed for the purchase price. As discussed earlier, the lender gives the buyer cash to pay the seller, and the buyer gives the lender a promissory note. The buyer also gives the lender a security instrument (mortgage or deed of trust) under which she pledges the property as collateral. When the transaction is complete, the buyer has the title recorded in her name and the lender has a lien recorded on the property.

> Some liens are statutory, that is, they become a lien automatically as a matter of law, even if the liens are not recorded. County property taxes, homeowners association dues, and water/sewer charges are typically a lien on a property to the extent they are unpaid. And, in most cases, these liens are first in line, even ahead of the mortgage liens.

What Is Foreclosure?

Foreclosure is the legal process of the mortgage holder taking the collateral for a promissory note in default. The process is slightly different from state to state, but there are basically two types of foreclosure: judicial and nonjudicial. In mortgage states, judicial foreclosure is used most often, whereas in deed of trust states, nonjudicial (called power of sale) foreclosure is used. Most states permit both types of proceedings, but it is common practice in most states to exclusively use one method or the other. A complete state-by-state list of foreclosure proceedings can be found in Appendix B.

Judicial Foreclosure

Judicial foreclosure is a lawsuit that the lender (mortgagee) brings against the borrower (mortgagor) to force the sale of the property. About one-third of the states use judicial foreclosure. Like all lawsuits, a judicial foreclosure starts with a summons (a legal notice of the lawsuit) served on the borrower and any other parties with inferior rights in the property. (Remember, all junior liens, including tenancies, are wiped out by the foreclosure, so they all need to be given legal notice of the proceeding.)

If the borrower does not file an answer to the lawsuit, the lender gets a judgment by default. A person is then appointed by the court to compute the total amount due including interest and attorney's fees. The lender then must advertise a notice of sale in the newspaper for several weeks.

If the total amount due is not paid by the sale date, a public sale is held on the courthouse steps. The entire process can take as little as a few months to a year depending on your state and the volume of court cases in your county.

The sale is conducted like an auction, in that the property goes to the highest bidder. Unless there is significant equity in the property, the only bidder at the sale will be a representative of the lender. The lender can bid up to the amount it is owed, without having to actually come out of pocket with cash to purchase the property. Once the lender has ownership of the property, it will try to sell it through a real estate agent.

If the proceeds from the sale are insufficient to satisfy the amount owed to the lender, the lender may be entitled to a deficiency judgment against the borrower and anyone else who guaranteed the loan. Some states prohibit a lender from obtaining a deficiency judgment against a borrower (applies only to owner-occupied, not investor properties). In practice, few lenders seek a deficiency judgment against the borrower.

Nonjudicial Foreclosure

A majority of the states permit a lender to foreclose without a lawsuit, using what is commonly called a "power of sale." Upon default of the borrower, the lender simply files a notice of default and a notice of sale that is published in the newspaper. The entire process generally takes about 90 days.

What Is a Deficiency?

In order for a borrower to be held personally liable for a foreclosure deficiency, there must be recourse on the note. Most loans in the residential market are with recourse. If possible, particularly when dealing with seller-financed loans (see Chapter 9), have a corporate entity sign on the note in your place. A corporation or limited liability company (LLC) protects its business owners from personal liability for business obligations. Upon default, the lender's legal recourse will be against the property or the corporate entity, but not against you, the business owner.

Strict Foreclosure

Two states—New Hampshire and Connecticut—permit strict foreclosure, which does not require a sale. When the court proceeding is started, the borrower has a certain amount of time to pay what is owed. Once that date has passed, title reverts to the lender without the need for a sale.

Key Points

- A mortgage is actually two things—a note and a security instrument.

- Some states use a deed of trust as a security instrument.

- Liens are prioritized by recording date.

- Foreclosure processes differ from state to state.

CHAPTER 3

Understanding the Mortgage Loan Market

Neither a borrower nor a lender be; for loan oft loses both itself and friend.

–William Shakespeare

The mortgage business is a complicated and ever-changing industry. It is important that you understand how the mortgage market works and how the lenders make their profit. In doing so, you will gain an appreciation of loan programs and why certain loans are offered by certain lenders.

There are several categories of lenders that are discussed in this chapter, and many lenders will fit in more than one category. In addition, some categories of lending are more of a lending "style" than a lender category; this concept will make more sense after you finish reading this chapter.

Institutional Lenders

The first broad category of distinction is institutional versus private. Institutional lenders include commercial banks, savings and loans or thrifts, credit unions, mortgage banking companies, pension funds, and insurance companies. These lenders generally make loans based on the income and credit of the borrower, and they generally follow standard lending guidelines. Private lenders are individuals or small companies that do not have insured depositors and are generally not regulated by the federal government.

Primary versus Secondary Mortgage Markets

First, these markets should not be confused with first and second mortgages, which were discussed in Chapter 2. *Primary mortgage lenders* deal directly with the public. They *originate* loans, that is, they lend money directly to the borrower. Often referred to as the "retail" side of the business, lenders make a profit from loan processing fees, not from the interest paid on the loan.

Primary mortgage lenders generally lend money to consumers, then sell the mortgage notes (together in large packages, not one at a time) to investors on the *secondary mortgage market* to replenish their cash reserves.

Portfolio lenders don't sell their loans to the secondary market, but rather they keep the loans as part of their portfolio (some lenders sell part of their loans and keep others as part of their portfolio). As such, they don't necessarily need to conform their loans to guidelines established by the Federal National Mortgage Association (FNMA) or the Federal Home Loan Corporation (FHLMC). Small, local banks that portfolio their loans can be an investor's best friend, because they can bend the rules to suit that investor's needs.

Larger portfolio lenders can handle more loans, because they have more funds, but they are not as flexible as the small banks. Larger portfolio lenders can also give you an unlimited amount of loans, whereas FNMA/FHLMC lenders have limits on the number of loans they can give you (currently loans for nine properties, but these limits often change). The nation's larger portfolio lenders include World Savings, Washington Mutual, Wells Fargo, and Bank of America.

The largest buyers on the secondary market are FNMA (or "Fannie Mae"), the Government National Mortgage Association (GNMA, or "Ginnie Mae"), and the FHLMC (or "Freddie Mac"). Private financial

---

Why Sell the Loan?

Lenders sell loans for a variety of reasons. First, they want to maximize their cash reserves. By law, banks must have a minimum reserve, so if they lend all of their available cash, they can't do any more loans. Second, they want to minimize their risk of interest rate fluctuations in the market. Typically a lender can lend six times their cash reserves.

---

institutions such as banks, life insurance companies, private investors, and thrift associations also buy notes.

FNMA is a quasi-governmental agency (controlled by the government but owned by private shareholders) that buys pools of mortgage loans in exchange for mortgage-backed securities. GNMA is a division of the Department of Housing and Urban Development (HUD), a governmental agency. Because most loans are sold on the secondary mortgage market to FNMA, GNMA, or FHLMC, most primary mortgage lenders conform their loan documentation to these agencies' guidelines (known as a "conforming" loan). Although primary lenders sell the loans on the secondary mortgage market, many of the primary lenders will continue to collect payments and deal with the borrower, a process called *servicing*.

Mortgage Bankers versus Mortgage Brokers

Many consumers assume that "mortgage companies" are banks that lend their own money. In fact, a company that you deal with may be either a mortgage banker or a mortgage broker.

A *mortgage banker* is a direct lender; it lends you its own money, although it often sells the loan to the secondary market. Mortgage

Loan Servicing

Loan servicing is an immensely profitable business for mortgage banks and other lenders. Servicing involves collecting the loan payments, accounting for tax and insurance escrows, dealing with customer issues, and mailing notices to the customer and the Internal Revenue Service (IRS). The average fee charged for servicing is about ⅜ percent of the loan amount. This may not sound like much, but try multiplying it by a billion dollars!

bankers (also known as "direct lenders") sometimes retain servicing rights as well.

A *mortgage broker* is a middleman who does the loan shopping and analysis for the borrower and puts the lender and borrower together. Many of the lenders through which the broker finds loans do not deal directly with the public (hence the expression "wholesale lender").

Using a mortgage banker can save the fees of a middleman and can make the loan process easier. A mortgage banker can give you direct loan approval, whereas a broker gives you information second-hand. However, many mortgage banks are limited in what they can offer, which is essentially their own product. Recently, mortgage banks have also become brokers, thus providing you with options in both worlds. They can give you direct approval for their own loans, or can broker a loan to other investors. In addition, if you present your loan application in a poor light, you've already made a bad impression. I am not suggesting you lie or mislead a lender, but understand that presenting a loan to a lender is like presenting your taxes to the IRS. There are many ways to do it, all of which are valid and legal. Using a mortgage broker allows you to present a loan application to a different lender in a different light (and you are a "fresh" face).

A mortgage broker charges a fee for his or her service but has access to a wide variety of loan programs. He or she also may have knowledge of how to present your loan application to different lenders for approval. Some mortgage bankers also broker loans. As an investor, it is wise to have both a mortgage broker and a mortgage banker on your team.

Mortgage Brokering

Keep in mind that mortgage brokering is an unlicensed profession in some state. If there is no licensing agency to complain to in your state, make sure you have personal references before you do business with a mortgage broker. And, licensing may be different for consumer loans than for investor or commercial loans.

Conventional versus Nonconventional Loans

Conventional financing, by definition, is not insured or guaranteed by the federal government (see discussion of government loans later in this chapter). Conventional loans are generally broken into two categories: conforming and nonconforming. A *conforming loan* is one that conforms or adheres to strict Fannie Mae/Freddie Mac loan underwriting guidelines.

Conforming Loans

Conforming loans are a low risk to the lender, so they offer the lowest interest rates. Conforming loans also have the strictest underwriting guidelines.

Conforming loans have the following three basic requirements:

1. *Borrower must have a minimum of debt.* Lenders look at the ratio of your monthly debt to income (debt-to-income ratio). Your regular monthly expenses (including mortgage payments, property taxes, insurance) should total no more than 33 percent to 38 percent of your gross monthly income (called "front-end ratio"). Furthermore, your monthly expenses plus other long-term debt payments (e.g., student loan, automobile, alimony, child support) should total no more than 36 percent of your gross monthly income (40% and in some cases 45%. If it is an FHA loan this can go as high as 50%.) These ratios can sometimes be increased if the borrower has excellent credit or puts up a larger down payment. Over the past several years these percentages have increased as more money has become available and competition has increased among lenders. When the loan default rates start to increase, lenders often react by tightening (lowering) the DTI ratios. When this happens borrowers need to show more income to qualify, thus borrowing less money and ultimately paying less for houses. In this fashion, lending practices can change the housing market even though there is no change in interest rates.

2. *Good credit rating.* You must be current on payments. Lenders will also require a certain minimum credit score (discussed in Chapter 4).

3. *Funds to close.* You must have the requisite down payment (generally 20 percent of the purchase price, although lenders often bend this rule), proof of where it came from, and a few months of cash reserves in the bank.

    In recent years, lenders have become liberal about down payment guidelines. Borrowers with better credit can generally get away with no down payment on their personal residence, although investors generally are required to put at least 20 percent down and show cash reserves. It is well-advised that

> ## Underwriting
>
> Underwriting is the task of applying guidelines that provide standards for determining whether or not a loan should be approved. Understand that loan approval is the final step in the loan application process before the money is handed over (known as "funding" a loan). Note that many lenders will give "preapproval" of a loan. Preapproval is really a half-baked commitment. Until a loan is approved in writing, the bank has no legal commitment to fund. And, in many cases, loan approval is often given with conditions attached that must be satisfied before closing.
>
> Every loan that is underwritten has a preliminary approval with conditions. As a matter of practice for an investor, ask the loan officer if you can see the underwriting approval letter with the conditions required for closing. You will know if is valid is there is a loan number attached to the condition sheet.

an investor keep a reserve of approximately 25 percent of the monthly mortgage payment for vacancies and repairs, particularly if he or she has several properties. This is where most investors get in trouble. While it is possible to purchase with no money down, someone needs to make the payments and have reserves for unexpected events.

FHA-insured loans (discussed later in this chapter) allow higher LTVs but are more limited in scope and are not generally available to investors (discussed later in this chapter).

Private mortgage insurance. Private mortgage insurance (PMI) requirements apply only to first mortgage loans; thus, you can get around PMI requirements by borrowing a first and second mortgage loan. So long as the first mortgage loan is less than 80 percent loan-to-value,

PMI is not required. However, the second mortgage loan may have a high interest rate, so that the blending of the interest rate on the first and second mortgage loans exceeds what you would be paying with a first mortgage and PMI. Use a calculator to figure out which is more profitable for you (the formula for interest rate blending is discussed in Chapter 5). Many lenders have eliminated private mortgage insurance by increasing the interest rates on loans above 80 percent LTV.

What Is the Loan-to-Value (LTV) Ratio?

Loan-to-value ratio is the percentage of the value of the property the lender is willing to lend. For example, if the property is worth $100,000, an 80 percent LTV loan will be for $80,000. Note that LTV is not the same as loan-to-purchase price, because the purchase price may be more or less than the appraised value (discussed in more detail in Chapter 5).

One way around the large down payment is to purchase PMI. Also known as "mortgage guaranty insurance," PMI will cover the lender's additional risk for a high loan-to-value ratio (LTV) program. The insurer will reimburse the lender for its additional risk of the high LTV. A high LTV loan will generally require a higher interest rate because of the increased risk to the lender. In recent years, PMI loans have become less common because PMI is not generally deductible. Congress approved a new bill for 2007 that will qualify allow deduction of PMI on loans originated in 2007. Consult your tax advisor for details.

PMI should not be confused with mortgage life insurance, which pays the borrower's loan balance in full when he or she dies (not recommended—regular term life insurance is a better deal for the money).

Nonconforming Loans

Nonconforming loans have no set guidelines and vary widely from lender to lender. In fact, lenders often change their own nonconforming guidelines from month to month.

Nonconforming loans are also known as "subprime" loans, because the target customer (borrower) has credit and/or income verification that is less than perfect. The subprime loans are often rated according to the creditworthiness of the borrower—"A," "B," "C," or "D."

An "A" credit borrower has had few or no credit problems within the past two years, with the exception of a late payment or two with a good explanation. A "C" credit borrower may have a history of several late payments and a bankruptcy.

The subprime loan business has grown enormously over the past ten years, particularly in the refinance business and with investor loans. Every lender has its own criteria for subprime loans, so it is impossible to list every loan program available on the market. Suffice it to say, the guidelines for subprime loans are much more lax than they are for conforming loans.

Will Subprime Loans Go Away?

Because of the rash of recent foreclosures, there has been talk that subprime lending may tighten up again, making it harder for people with low income and/or bad credit to buy a new home. The risk of default may be too much for some lenders to handle, which means fewer lenders will work this market, reducing competition and resulting in higher rates. Inevitably, lending programs tend to go in cycles, with lenders being more lax in good real estate markets and tightening up their guidelines in bad markets. When housing prices are up, even risky loans work out because borrowers with equity have more options to either sell or refinance when they get into trouble. When housing prices are down, defaults increase, particularly for those who barely qualified for the loan in the first place.

Government Loan Programs

The federal government and state governments sponsor loan programs to encourage home ownership. Most of the loan programs are geared towards low-income neighborhoods and first-time homebuyers. If you are dealing in low-income properties, you should be aware of these guidelines if you intend to sell properties to these target homebuyers. Also, some of these programs are geared to investors as well.

Federal Housing Administration Loans

HUD is the U.S. Department of Housing and Urban Development, an executive branch of the federal government. The Federal Housing Administration (FHA) is an arm of HUD that administers loan programs. HUD does not lend money but rather insures lenders that make high LTV loans. Because high LTV loans are risky for lenders, the FHA-insured loan programs cover the additional risk. Not all lenders can make FHA-insured loans; they must be approved by HUD.

Confusion of Terms

Some mortgage professionals will use the expression "conventional" to mean "conforming," and vice versa. So, when a mortgage broker says that "you'll have to go with a nonconforming loan," the loan documentation may still have to substantially conform with FNMA guidelines. In fact, even loans that do not conform with FNMA or conventional standards are underwritten on FNMA "paper" (the actual note, mortgage, and other related documents). Lenders do this with the intention of eventually selling the paper, even if it may begin as a portfolio loan.

The most common FHA loan program is the 203(b) program, designed for first-time homebuyers. This program allows an owner-occupant to put just 3 percent down and borrow 97 percent loan-to-value. The 3 percent down could come from another source with the borrower needing as little as $500 down. This program is for owner-occupied (noninvestor) properties, but investors should be familiar with the program because they may wish to sell a property to a buyer who may use the program.

The two most common HUD loans available for investors are the Title 1 Loan and the 203(k) loan.

Title 1 loan. The Title 1 loan insures loans of up to $25,000 for light to moderate rehab of single-family properties, or $12,000 per unit for a maximum of $60,000 on multifamily properties. The interest rates on these loans are generally market rate, although local participation by state or municipal agencies may reduce the rate (see below).

An interesting note on a Title 1 loans is that it is not limited to owners of the property. A lessee or equitable owner under an installment land contract (discussed in Chapter 9) may qualify for the loan.

FHA 203(k) loan. The 203(k) program is for an investor who wants to live in the home while rehabbing it. It allows the investor-occupant to borrow money for the purchase or refinance of a home as well as for the rehab costs. It is an excellent alternative to the traditional route for these investors, which is to buy a property with a temporary ("bridge") loan, fix the property, then refinance it (many lenders won't offer attractive, long-term financing on rehab properties).

The 203(k) loan can be for up to the value of the property plus anticipated improvement costs, or 110 percent of the value of the property, whichever is less. The rehab cost must be at least $5,000, but there is no limit to the size of the rehab (although it cannot be used for new construction, that is, the basic foundation of the property must be used, even if the building is razed). The program can be used for condominiums, provided that the condo project is otherwise FHA qualified. Cooperative apartments, popular in New York and California, are not eligible.

The Department of Veterans Affairs

The Department of Veterans Affairs (VA) guarantees certain loan programs for eligible veterans. As an occupant, an eligible veteran can borrow up to 100 percent of the purchase price of the property. When a borrower with a VA-guaranteed loan cannot meet the payments, the lender forecloses on the home. The lender next looks to the VA to cover the loss for its guarantee, and the VA takes ownership of the home. The VA then offers the property for sale to the public.

State and Local Loan Programs

Many states and localities sponsor programs to help first-time homebuyers qualify for mortgage loans. The programs are aimed at improving low-income neighborhoods by increasing the number of owners versus renters in the area. Most of these programs are for owner-occupants, not investors, but it may also help to know about these programs when you are selling homes.

Some state and local programs work in conjunction with HUD programs, such as Title 1 loans. Contact your state or city department of housing for more information on locally sponsored loan programs.

Condominium Financing Pitfalls

Condominiums can be difficult to finance in general, as compared to single-family homes. In general, stay away from units in developments that have a large concentration of investor-owners. Condo developments that have a 50 percent or more concentration of nonoccupant owners are very difficult to finance through institutional lenders.

A list of links to state programs can be found at <http://library. hsh.com/?row_id=63>.

Commercial Lenders

Most of the discussion so far has been about financing of single-family homes and small multifamily residential homes. What about large multifamily projects and commercial projects, such as shopping centers, strip malls, and office buildings? Many of the same concepts do apply, except for the financing guidelines.

Commercial lenders generally do not have industry-wide loan criteria. Instead, each lender has its own criteria and will review loans on a project-by-project basis. Lenders will look at the experience of the investor as well as the income and expenses of the particular collateral. In other words, commercial lenders are more concerned with whether the property will generate enough income to pay the loan, not whether the borrower has good credit (although a borrower with poor credit will generally have a hard time getting any type of loan from an institutional lender). A commercial appraisal is required, which is more detailed and expensive than a residential appraisal. A commercial loan will require the borrower to have a substantial reserve of cash to handle vacancies.

Commercial loans also can be made for residential buildings of five units or more, but there is a minimum loan amount required by each lender (generally a $300,000 to $500,000, depending on the property values in your marketplace). Oddly enough, multimillion dollar loans are often made without recourse to the borrower. In other words, if the project fails, the borrower (often a corporate entity) is not liable for the debt. The lender's sole recourse is to foreclose against the property. For this reason, the lender is more concerned with the property than the borrower.

Key Points

- Most lenders sell their loans to the secondary market.

- Loans come in three basic categories: conforming, nonconforming, and government.

- The government does not lend money, but rather it guarantees loans.

- Commercial lenders look to the property rather than the borrower.

CHAPTER 4

Working with Lenders

Except for the con men borrowing money they shouldn't get and the widows who have to visit with the handsome young men in the trust department, no sane person ever enjoyed visiting a bank.

–Martin Meyer

Now that you understand how loans and the mortgage market works you can begin to understand how to approach financing. In Chapter 3, we discussed a variety of loan *programs* that differ based on the lender, the type of property, and the borrower. We will now turn to loan *types* that are generally available in most of the loan programs discussed thus far and the advantages and disadvantages of each. Before doing so, let's explore some of the relevant issues we need to consider when borrowing money.

Interest Rate

The cost of borrowing money, that is, the interest rate, is one of the most important factors. As discussed in Chapter 1, interest rates affect monthly payments, which in turn affect how much you can afford to pay for a property. It may also affect cash flow, which affects your decision to hold or sell property.

Loan Amortization

There are many different ways a loan can be structured as far as interest payments go. The most common ways are simple interest and amortized.

As discussed in Chapter 1, a simple interest loan is calculated by multiplying the loan balance by the interest rate. So, for example, a $100,000 loan at 12 percent interest would be $12,000 per year, or $1,000 per month. The payments here, of course, represent interest-only, so the principal amount of the loan does not change.

An amortized loan is slightly more involved. Simply stated, an amortized loan means that a loan has equal payments for a certain period of time (e.g., monthly for 30 years) and at the end of that time the loan will be paid to a zero balance. The actual mathematical formula is beyond a book like this, so we've provided a sample interest rate table in Appendix A. However, you can find a thousand Internet Web sites that will do the calculations instantly online (try mine at <http://realestate.yahoo.com>—click on "calculators"). The amortization method breaks down payments over a number of years, with the payment remaining constant each month. However, the interest is calculated on the remaining balance, so the amount of each monthly payment accounts for principal and interest changes. For the most part, the more payments you make, the more you decrease the amount of principal owed (the amount of the loan still left to pay). See Figure 4.1.

The loan *term* or duration is important to figuring your payment. By custom, most loans are amortized over 30 years or 360 monthly payments. The second most common loan term is 15 years. The payments on a 15-year amortization are higher each month, but you pay the loan off faster and thus pay less interest in the long run.

FIGURE 4.1 Amortization of $100,000 Loan at 8% Interest Over 30 Years

Payment #	Date	Payment	Interest	Principal	Loan Balance
1	02-01-2003	733.76	666.67	67.09	99,932.91
2	03-01-2003	733.76	666.22	67.54	99,865.37
3	04-01-2003	733.76	665.77	67.99	99,797.38
4	05-01-2003	733.76	665.32	68.44	99,728.94
5	06-01-2003	733.76	664.86	68.90	99,660.04
6	07-01-2003	733.76	664.40	69.36	99,590.68
7	08-01-2003	733.76	663.94	69.82	99,520.86
8	09-01-2003	733.76	663.47	70.29	99,450.57
9	10-01-2003	733.76	663.00	70.76	99,379.81
10	11-01-2003	733.76	662.53	71.23	99,308.58
11	12-01-2003	733.76	662.06	71.70	99,236.88
12	01-01-2004	733.76	661.58	72.18	99,164.70
13	02-01-2004	733.76	661.10	72.66	99,092.04
14	03-01-2004	733.76	660.61	73.15	99,018.89
15	04-01-2004	733.76	660.13	73.63	98,945.26
16	05-01-2004	733.76	659.64	74.12	99,871.14
17	06-01-2004	733.76	659.14	74.62	98,796.52
18	07-01-2004	733.76	658.64	75.12	98,721.40
19	08-01-2004	733.76	658.14	75.62	98,645.78
20	09-01-2004	733.76	657.64	76.12	98,569.66
21	10-01-2004	733.76	657.13	76.63	98,493.03
22	11-01-2004	733.76	656.62	77.14	98,415.89
23	12-01-2004	733.76	656.11	77.65	98,338.24
24	01-01-2005	733.76	655.59	78.17	98,260.07
25	02-01-2005	733.76	655.07	78.69	98,181.18
26	03-01-2005	733.76	654.54	79.22	98,102.16
27	04 01 2005	733.76	654.01	79.75	98,022.41
28	05-01-2005	733.76	653.48	80.28	97,942.13
29	06-01-2005	733.76	652.95	80.81	97,861.32
30	07-01-2005	733.76	652.41	81.35	97,779.97
31	08-01-2005	733.76	651.87	81.89	97,698.08
32	09-01-2005	733.76	651.32	82.44	97,615.64
33	10-01-2005	733.76	650.77	82.99	97,532.65
34	11-01-2005	733.76	650.22	83.54	97,449.11
35	12-01-2005	733.76	649.66	84.10	97,365.01
36	01-01-2006	733.76	649.10	84.66	97,280.35
37	02-01-2006	733.76	648.54	85.22	97,195.13
38	03-01-2006	733.76	647.97	85.79	97,109.34
39	04-01-2006	733.76	647.40	86.36	97,022.98
40	05-01-2006	733.76	646.82	86.94	96,936.04
41	06-01-2006	733.76	646.24	87.52	96,848.52
42	07-01-2006	733.76	645.66	88.10	96,760.42
43	08-01-2006	733.76	645.07	88.69	96,671.73
44	09-01-2006	733.76	644.48	89.28	96,582.45
45	10-01-2006	733.76	643.88	89.88	96,492.57
46	11-01-2006	733.76	643.28	90.48	96,402.09
349	02-01-2032	733.76	56.28	677.48	7,764.01
350	03-01-2032	733.76	51.76	682.00	7,082.01
351	04-01-2032	733.76	47.21	686.55	6,395.46
352	05-01-2032	733.76	42.64	691.12	5,704.34
353	06-01-2032	733.76	38.03	695.73	5,008.61
354	07-01-2032	733.76	33.39	700.37	4,308.24
355	08-01-2032	733.76	28.72	705.04	3,603.20
356	09-01-2032	733.76	24.02	709.74	2,893.46
357	10-01-2032	733.76	19.29	714,47	2,178.99
358	11-01-2032	733.76	14.53	719.23	1,459.76
359	12-01-2032	733.76	9.73	724.03	735.73

15-Year Amortization versus 30-Year Amortization

In general, 15-year loans tend to have a slightly lower interest rate. In addition, you reach your financial goal of "free and clear" faster. However, there are three downsides to the 15-year loan. The first is that you are obligated to a higher payment that reduces your cash flow. Second, the higher monthly obligation appears on your credit report, which affects your debt ratios and thus your ability to borrow more money (discussed later in this chapter). Third, your monthly payment is less interest and more principal. While this may sound like a good thing, it doesn't give you the same tax benefits; interest payments are deductible, principal payments are not.

Three Negatives to a 15-Year Loan

1. Higher monthly payments
2. Increased debt ratios
3. Less of a tax deduction

Unless the interest rate on the 15-year note is significantly lower, opt for the 30-year note. You can accomplish the faster principal paydown by making extra interest payments to the lender.

☛ **Example:** On a $100,000 loan amortized at 8% over 30 years, your payment is $733.76. If you make an additional principal payment each month of $100, the loan would be fully amortized in just over 20 years, saving you $62,468.87 in interest.

You can use a financial calculator to calculate how much extra you need to pay each month to reduce the loan term (again, try mine at <http://realestate.yahoo.com/>—click on "calculators"). And, of course, when times are hard and the property is vacant, you aren't obligated to make the higher payment.

Biweekly Mortgage Payment Programs

An entire multilevel marketing business has been made out of selling people the idea of a biweekly mortgage program. Basically, if you pay your loan every two weeks rather than monthly, you make two extra payments per year. With the additional payments going towards principal, the debt amortizes faster. Before plunking down several hundred dollars to a third party to do this for you, ask your lender. Many lenders will set up a direct deposit program from your bank account for biweekly payments.

Interest-Only Loans

Over the past several years, many loans obtained by borrowers (both investor and owner-occupied) have been interest-only. An interest-only payment is lower than a corresponding 30-year amortized loan with the same interest rate.

Amortized loans payments are generally fixed for the life of the loan, whereas most interest-only loans have adjustable rates that are fixed for the first few years.

It is important to understand interest-only loans and how to use them. The common myth is that interest-only loans are bad because the debt is never paid back. As you can see from figure 4.1, the payments on a 30-year amortized loan are mostly interest in the first few years. Thus, the difference in total payments and total principal paid on a 30-year loan versus an interest-only loan are not substantial over a three-year period. If the investor only intends to keep the loan for a few years, then the lower payments of an interest-only loan may make sense.

Some lenders are offering 40 and 50 amortized loans that are the equivalent of interest-only loans in terms of monthly payments. There's no right answer, so you need to do the math to see what is the difference between these loans and how you use them to your advantage.

Balloon Mortgage

A *balloon* is a premature end to a loan's life. For example, a loan could call for interest-only payments for three years, then be due in full at the end of three years. Or, a loan could be amortized over 30 years, with the principal balance remaining due in five years. When the loan balloon payment becomes due, the borrower must pay the full amount or face foreclosure.

A balloon provision can be risky for the borrower, but if used with common sense, it may work effectively by satisfying the lender's needs. Balloon notes are often used by builders as a short-term financing tool. These types of loans are also known as "bridge" or "mezzanine" financing.

Reverse Amortization

Regular amortization means as you make payments the loan balance decreases. Reverse amortization means the more you pay, the more you owe. How is that possible? Simple—by making a lower payment each month than would be possible for the stated interest rate. A reverse amortization loan increases your cash flow but also increases your risk because you will owe more in the future. If you bought the property below market, a reverse amortization loan may make sense, especially if real estate prices are rising rapidly (another option may be a variable rate loan, discussed later in this chapter).

> ### Reverse Amortization Loans for the Elderly
>
> Many mortgage banks are advertising reverse am-ortization loans to elderly homeowners as a way to reduce their monthly payments. Most of these loan programs are not intended for investors as described above.

Property Taxes and Insurance Escrows

In addition to monthly principal and interest payments on your loan, you'll have to figure on paying property taxes and hazard insurance. Many lenders won't trust you to make these payments on your own, especially if you are borrowing at a high loan-to-value (80 percent LTV or higher). Lenders estimate the annual payments for taxes and insurance, then collect these payments from you monthly into a reserve account (called an "escrow" or "impound account"). The lender then makes the disbursements directly to the county tax collector and your insurance company on an annual basis. Thus, the total amount collected each month consists of principal and interest payments on the note, plus taxes and insurance—hence the acronym PITI.

Loan Costs

Origination Fee

The cost of a loan is as important as the interest rate. Lenders and mortgage brokers charge various fees for giving you a loan (and you thought they just made money on the interest rates!). Traditionally, the most expensive part of the loan package is the loan origination fee. The fee is expressed in *points,* that is, a percentage of the loan amount: 1 point = 1 percent. So, for example, if a lender charges a "1 point origination fee" on a $100,000 loan, you would pay 1 percent, or $1,000, as a fee.

> ### Tax Deductions and Points
>
> An origination fee is not deductible in the tax year you get your loan, but must be deducted over the life of your loan. A discount point is consider pre-paid interest, so it is deductible in the tax year you get the loan. Remember, if you pay off your loan early (as most loans are), you can deduct the balance of the origination fee that you have not yet deducted in the tax year you sell or refinance the property.

Discount Points

Another built-in profit center is the charging of "discount points." The lender will offer you a lower interest rate for the payment of money up front. Thus, if you want your interest rate to be lower, you can "buy down" the rate by paying ½ point (percent) or more of the loan up front. Buying down the rate only makes sense if you plan on keeping the loan for a long time; otherwise buying down the interest rate is a waste of money.

Borrowers nowadays are smarter and try to beat the banks at their own game by refusing to pay points. Banks even advertise "no cost" loans, that is, loans with no discount points or origination fees.

Yield Spread Premiums: The Little Secret Your Lender Doesn't Want You to Know

The lower the interest rate, the better off you are, or are you? Lenders advertise "wholesale" interest rates on a daily basis to mortgage brokers, who then advertise rates to their customers. This wholesale interest rate can be marked up on the retail side by the mortgage broker.

☞ **Example:** Say, for example, your mortgage broker offers you an interest rate of 7.25% on a $200,000, 30-year fixed loan. The monthly payment on this loan would be $1,364.35, which is acceptable to you. However, the wholesale rate offered by the lender may be 7.00%, which is $1,330.60 per month. This difference may not seem like much, but over 30 years, it amounts to about $12,000 in additional interest paid. The mortgage broker receives a "bonus" back from the lender for the additional interest earned. This bonus is called a yield spread premium (YSP) because it represents the additional yield earned by the lender for the higher interest rate.

Are Yield Spread Premiums Legal?

At this time, YSPs are legal as long as they are disclosed on the loan documents. Although it is not technically a fee to the borrower, YSPs are not illegal "kickbacks" to the mortgage broker either. You will, however, see the fee noted on the HUD-1 closing statement as POC (paid outside of closing).

Keep in mind that the disclosure is only noted if you used a mortgage broker. If you use a direct lender, it is not disclosed.

Another new fee that lenders sometimes earn, but don't report, is a service release premium (SRP). As discussed in chapter three, loan servicing is a profitable business for lenders in simply collecting payments on loans each month for other lenders. A lender that buys a loan from another lender may pay a fee for getting the rights to service the loan themselves.

Loan Junk Fees

Even without points and at par (no markup on the interest rate), there is no such thing as a no-cost loan. Lenders sneak in their profit by disguising other fees, such as the following:

- Administrative Review

- Underwriting Charge

- Documentation Fee

These charges are given fancy names but are really just ways for the lender to make more profit. Lenders also pad their actual fees, such as the cost of obtaining credit reports, courier charges, and other "miscellaneous fees" (one lender admitted to me that he pays less than $15 for a credit report yet charges the borrower $85!). Understand that lenders are in business to make money, so if a loan sounds too good to be true, it probably is—look carefully at their fees and charges.

Good Faith Estimate

By law, a lender is required to give you a list of the loan fees up front when you apply for the loan. Unscrupulous lenders are notorious for adding in last-minute charges and fees that you won't discover until closing. Of course, you are free to back out at that point, but who wants to lose a good real estate deal? Lenders know this reality, so make sure you get as much as you can in writing before closing the loan.

"Standard" Loan Costs

While every lender has its own fees and points it charges, there are certain costs you can expect to pay with every loan transaction. These fees should be listed in the lender's good faith estimate as well as on the second page of the closing statement. The closing statement is prepared at closing by the escrow agent on a form known as a HUD-1, in compliance with the Real Estate Settlement Procedures Act (RESPA), a federal law. A sample of this form can be found in Appendix C. All of the following charges appear on page two of the form:

- *Title insurance policy.* While a lender secures its loan with a security instrument recorded against the property, it wants a guarantee that its lien is in first position (or, in the case of a second mortgage, second position). A lender's policy of title insurance guarantees to the lender it is in first position (or, in the case of a second mortgage, second position). This policy costs anywhere from a few hundred dollars to a thousand dollars, depending on the amount of the loan and when the last time a title insurance policy was issued on the property; the more recently another policy was issued, the cheaper the policy. Also, if you are purchasing an owner's title insurance policy in conjunction with the lender's policy (very common), the fee for the lender's policy is substantially reduced.

- *Prepaid interest.* While this is not a "fee," it is a cost of financing you pay up front. Because interest is paid for the use of money the month before, you need to figure on paying pro-rated interest. For example, let's assume your monthly payment on the mortgage note will be $1,000. If you close your loan on the 15th of the month, your first payment won't be due for 45 days. The lender will collect 15 days of interest at closing for the use of the money that month, which is $500.

- *Application fee.* While standard among some lenders, this fee is really a "junk" fee. Nobody should charge you for asking you to do business with them. Lenders often waive this fee if they fund your loan.

- *Document recording fees.* Because the mortgage or deed of trust will be recorded at the county, there are fees charged. The usual range is about $5 to $10 per page, and the typical FNMA mortgage or deed of trust is anywhere from 12 to 20 pages. In addition, some states and localities (e.g., New York) charge an additional tax on mortgage transactions based on the amount of the loan.

- *Reserves.* If the lender is escrowing property taxes and insurance, it will generally collect a few months extra up front. While technically not a cost, it is cash out of your pocket.

- *Closing fee.* The lender, company, attorney, or escrow company that closes the loan charges a fee for doing so. Closing a loan involves preparing a closing statement, accounting for the monies, and passing around the papers. The closer actually sits down with the borrower and explains the documents and, in most cases, takes a notary's acknowledgment of the borrower (a mortgage or deed of trust must be executed before a notary in order for it to be accepted for recording in public records; the promissory note is not recorded but held by the lender until it is paid in full). The closer also makes sure the documents find their way back to the lender or the county for recording.

- *Appraisal.* Virtually all loans require an appraisal to verify value. An appraisal will cost you between $300 and $500, and even more if the subject property is a multiunit or commercial building. Appraisers often charge additional fees for a "rent survey," which is a sampling of rent payments of similar properties. The lender will want this information to verify that the property can sustain the income you projected.

(FNMA Form 2007, copy of which can be found in the appendix of this book, adds a few hundred bucks to the appraisal cost.)

- *Credit report.* Lenders charge a fee for running your credit report. The lender may charge as much as $85 for a full credit report. Vendors often run short-form credit reports, which are much cheaper. The lender may run a short-form version first to get a quick look at your credit, then a full report at a later time (called a "three bureau merge" because it contains information from the three major credit bureaus).

- *Survey.* A lender may require that a survey be done of the property. A *survey* is a drawing that shows where the property lies in relation to the nearest streets or landmarks. It will also show where the buildings and improvements on the property sit in relation to the boundaries. If a recent survey was performed, it may not be necessary to do a new survey. Rather, the lender may ask for a survey update from the same surveyor or another surveyor. In some parts of the country, an "Improvement Location Certificate" is used; it is essentially a drive-by survey.

- *Document preparation fees.* Some lenders will charge you an attorney's fee for document preparation. Larger lenders have in-house attorneys and paralegals. Smaller lenders hire outside service companies to prepare the loan documents. The reason documents are not always done "in house" is because of the complexities of compliance with lending regulations. Document preparation companies pay lawyers to research the laws and draft documents for compliance. Based on the information provided by the lender, the document preparation company prepares the forms for the lender. The fee for this service is generally a few hundred dollars, which is passed on to the borrower.

Now that you know how lenders make their money, you can negotiate your loan with confidence. Virtually every fee a lender asks for can be negotiated. However, don't expect the lender to waive every fee, charge no points, and get no back-end fees (yield spread premiums). The lender has to make a profit to be willing to do business with you. Profit is also important to you as an investor, but so is the availability of the money you borrow. If you want a lender that is willing to work hard for you, make sure you are willing to pay reasonable compensation. Pinching pennies with your lender will not get it excited about pushing your loan through the process faster. However, knowing what fees are negotiable will allow you to get a loan at a fair interest rate and pay a reasonable fee to get it.

RESPA (Real Estate Settlement and Procedures Act) requires that fees charged to a borrower are actual fees and not padded. You can ask for a receipt from any vendor that is on the HUD to confirm it is an actual invoice. The broker can charge his own "junk" fee that is negotiable, such as processing, underwriter review, servicing review, and almost any item that has the name "review."

Risk

In addition to profit and cash flow, one of the major factors you should consider in borrowing money is risk. While maximum leverage is important to the investor, it is also higher risk to the investor. The more money you borrow, the more risk you could potentially incur. That is, while you have less investment to lose, you may be personally liable for the debt you have incurred.

With larger commercial projects, the lender's main concern is the financial viability of the project itself. In that case, the borrower does not necessarily have to sign personally on the promissory note. The lender's sole legal recourse is to foreclose the property.

With smaller residential loans, the investor/borrower signs personally on the note and is thus liable personally for the obligation. While the lender can foreclose the property, there may be a deficiency owed that is the personal obligation of the borrower. In the late 1980s, many leveraged investors learned this lesson the hard way when they were forced to file for bankruptcy protection. A smart investor finances properties with a cash cushion, positive (or at least breakeven) cash flow, and at a reasonable loan-to-value ratio.

Nothing Down

While "nothing-down" financing is viable, it does not necessarily mean a 100 percent loan-to-value. For example, buying a $150,000 property for $150,000 with all borrowed money is not a bad deal if the property is worth $200,000. That's a 75 percent LTV. Buying a property for close to 100 percent of its value and financing it 100 percent with personal recourse is very risky. If you don't have the means to support the payments while the property is vacant, you may be in for trouble. Like any business, real estate is about maintaining cash flow.

So, in considering your loan, factor in the following issues:

- Are you near the top of an inflated market?

- Is the local economy's outlook good or bad?

- If purchasing, are you buying below market?

- How long do you intend to hold the property and for what purposes?

- Are prices likely to drop before you sell it?

- Will you be able to refinance the property in the future?

- Are you personally obligated on the note, or is the debt nonrecourse (or signed for by your corporate entity)?

All of these factors are relevant to risk and to whether you want to leverage yourself without a backup plan.

Loan Types

In Chapter 3, we discussed broad categories of loans, such as conventional versus government loans, conforming versus nonconforming loans, brokered loans versus portfolio loans, etc. These distinctions are really lending "styles" more than loan types. Virtually every lender or loan category involves variation of the loan term and interest rate. The loan term is the length of time by which the loan is amortized. The loan term is fixed, whereas the interest rate can vary throughout the term of the loan. Each loan type (fixed versus variable interest rate, 15-year versus 30-year) has a place for the borrower/ investor, and we will explore the benefits and detriments of each.

The most common type of real estate loan is a fixed-rate, 30-year amortization. A fixed-rate loan is desirable because it provides certainty. It hedges your bet against higher interest rates by allowing you to lock in a low interest rate. If interest rates fall, you can always refinance at a lower rate at a later time.

With interest rates uncertain in the future, many lenders are offering variable-rate financing. Known as an adjustable-rate mortgage (ARM), there are dozens of variations to suit the lender's profit motives and borrower's needs.

ARMs have two limits, or caps, on the rate increase. One cap regulates the limit on interest rate increases over the life of the loan; the other limits the amount the interest rate can be increased at a time. For example, if the initial rate is 6 percent, it may have a lifetime cap of 11 percent and a one-time cap of 2 percent. The adjustments are made monthly, every six months, once a year, or once every few years, depending on the "index" on which the ARM is based. An index is an outside source that can be determined by formulas, such as the following:

- LIBOR (London Interbank Offered Rate)—based on the interest rate at which international banks lend and borrow funds in the London Interbank market.

- COFI (Cost of Funds Index)—based on the 11th District's Federal Home Loan Bank of San Francisco. These loans often adjust on a monthly basis, which can make bookkeeping a real headache!

- T-bills Index—based on average rates the federal government pays on U.S. treasury bills. Also known as the Treasury Constant Maturity, or TCM.

- CD Index (certificate of deposit)—based on average rates banks are paying on six-month CDs.

The index you choose will affect how long your rate is fixed for and the chances that your interest rate will increase. Which one is best? Because that depends on what is going on in the national and world economy, you have to review your short-term and long-term goals with your lender before choosing an index.

ARMs are very common in the subprime market and with portfolio lenders, but they can be very risky because of the uncertainty of future interest rates. ARM loans have gotten a bad reputation in recent years because many people bought properties with lower payments, then couldn't afford the payment when the rate adjusted. Some bought with the assumption that property values would increase, rates would stay the same, or that they would make more money in the future. In many cases, these assumptions proved to be incorrect. However, like a balloon mortgage, an ARM can be used effectively with a little common sense. If you plan to sell or refinance the property within a few years, then an ARM may make sense, but you can't rely on too many assumptions. If you get a good price on a property and hit the market on an upswing, an ARM loan could prove to be a smart financing tool.

Hybrid ARM

Ask your lender about a hybrid ARM, that is, an ARM that is fixed for a period of three, five, seven, or even ten years. After that time, the rate will adjust, usually once (hence the expression "3/1 ARM" or "5/1 ARM"). The initial rates on these loans are not as good as a six-month ARM but will give you more flexibility and certainty (generally, the longer the rate is fixed for, the higher interest rate you'll pay—these rates are based on the 10-year treasury bond rate). Also, watch for prepayment penalties that are often built into ARM loans.

For more information on ARM loans, you can download the official consumer pamphlet prepared by the Federal Reserve Board and the Office of Thrift Supervision at my Web site, <www.legalwiz. com/arm>.

One of the most misunderstood loans is called the option ARM. With an ARM, the interest rate is based on an index like the London Interbank Offered Rate (LIBOR). The loan has four payment options, each of which can change monthly, based on the interest rate the loan is indexed to.

These options are:

- interest only,

- amortized for 15 years,

- amortized for 30 years, or

- minimum payment.

Depending on the market interest rate, the minimum payment may create a negative amortization, which means the loan balance may increase with time. Carefully used, an option ARM can be an excellent way to hedge your bets with rental properties. How? Because this provides a low-payment option if you have unexpected repairs or vacancies. The option ARM is particularly effective in a rising market because it gives you some breathing room if your loan balance is increasing.

Choosing a Lender

Choosing a lender that you want to work with involves several factors, not the least of which is an open mind. You need a lender that can bend the rules a little when you need it and get the job done on a deadline. You need a lender that is large enough to have pull, but small enough to give you personal attention. And, most of all, you need a lender that can deliver what it promises.

Prepayment Penalties

Lenders are smart investors, too. If interest rates are falling, lenders don't want you to pay off a higher-interest-rate loan. They discourage you from refinancing by adding a prepayment penalty (PPP) clause to your loan. The PPP provision states that if you pay the loan in full within a certain time period (usually within one year to three years), you must pay a penalty. The common penalty ranges from 1 percent to 6 percent of the original loan balance. Make sure that your loan does not have a PPP if you plan on refinancing or selling the property in the next few years.

There are two types of prepayment penalties; soft and hard. Soft prepayment penalty means that if you refinance the property you pay up to 6 months' interest as a penalty. However, if you sell the property to a third party there is no prepayment penalty. Hard prepayment means that you pay six months interest whether you refinance or sell. Lenders typically have 6-month, 2-year, 3-year and 5 year; soft and hard prepayment penalties. They price loans based on these penalties with interest rates less the longer the prepayment penalties. There are times as an investor that you know that you are going to keep the property for a longer term and the prepayment penalty makes sense because the interest rate on the loan could be as much as 1/2 percent less. Discuss this option with your mortgage professional to determine the best loan based on you circumstances. And, no matter what your mortgage broker says, read the documents carefully at closing. Many investors get tricked into signing documents with a prepayment penalty. When they realize the mistake, it's often too late, so beware!

Length of Time in Business

Because the mortgage brokering business is not highly regulated in most states, there are a lot of fly-by-night operations. Bad news travels faster than good news in business, so bad mortgage brokers don't last too long. Look for a company that has been in business for a few years. Check out the company's history with your local better business bureau. If mortgage brokers are licensed with your state, check to see if any complaints or investigations were made against them.

Also, ask for referrals from other investors and real estate agents. Many mortgage brokers will bait you with "too good to be true" loan programs that most investors won't qualify for. Once they have you hooked, it may be too late to switch brokers, and now you are forced to take whatever loan they can find for you. It's not that all of these mortgage brokers are crooks; it's often the case that the broker is just not knowledgeable about the particular loan programs they offer. In many cases, the particular lender they were dealing with was the culprit. Many wholesale lenders offer programs to mortgage brokers, then when the loan comes through, the underwriter changes its mind or asks for more documentation. In some cases, it is the old bait and switch; in other cases, it is simply a miscommunication between the wholesale lender and the mortgage broker. Thus, it is important that you ask the mortgage broker if it has dealt with the particular lender or loan program in the past.

Company Size

A company that is too big can be problematic because of high employee turnaround. Also, the proverbial "buck" gets passed around a lot. If you are dealing with a mortgage broker, it is often a one-person operation. Dealing with a one-man operation may be good in terms of communication if he or she is a go-getter. On the other hand, the individual may be hard to get a hold of, because he or she is answering the phone all day.

Six Questions to Ask Your Lender

1. How many regular investor clients do you have?
2. Do you get any back-end fees from the lender?
3. What percentage of your loans don't get funded (completed)?
4. What kind of special nonconforming loan programs do you have for investors?
5. What income and credit requirements do I need?
6. What documentation will I need to supply you with?

A small to midsized company is a good bet. You will be able to get the boss on the phone, but he or she will have a good support staff to handle the minor details. Also, a midsized company may have access to more wholesale lenders than a one-person company.

Experience in Investment Properties

It is important to deal with a mortgage broker or banker that has experience with investor loans. Owner-occupant loans are entirely different than investor loans. And, it is important that the broker or lender you are dealing with has a number of different programs. It is often the case that you find out a particular loan program won't work, in which case you need to switch lenders (or loan programs) in a heartbeat to meet a funding deadline.

How to Present the Deal to a Lender

For the most part, lenders follow guidelines established by FNMA and Freddie Mac, as well as their own lending guidelines. If you are looking for the best interest rate, then you must be able to conform to FNMA guidelines, which include a high credit score, provable income, and verifiable assets.

If you are not going with a conforming loan, then there are the following basic guidelines a lender will look at:

- Your credit score

- Your provable income

- The property itself

- Your down payment

Your Credit Score

Much of the institutional loan industry is driven by credit. While having spotless credit is not a necessity, it is certainly a good asset, if used wisely.

Your credit history is maintained primarily by three large companies, known as the credit bureaus: Equifax, TransUnion, and Experian (formerly TRW). Your credit report has "headers" that contain information about your addresses (every one they can find), phone numbers (even the unlisted ones), employer, Social Security number, aliases, and date of birth. This information is usually reported by banks and credit card companies that report to the credit bureaus (be careful about giving your unlisted address or phone number to your credit card company—it may end up on your credit file). Some information comes from public records, such as court filings and property records. You can obtain an annual free credit report from free credit report from www.freecreditreport.com. Every lender uses a different credit reporting agency, therefore each credit report will be different. Each credit reporting agency uses a different set of mathematical algorithms, thus changing FICO scores.

Your credit report also contains a history of nearly every charge card, loan, or other extension of credit that you ever had. It will show the type of loan (e.g., installment loan or revolving credit), the maximum you can borrow on the account, a history of payments, and the amount you currently owe. It will also show information from public records, such as judgments, IRS liens, and bankruptcy filings. Some debts are reported by collection agencies, such as unpaid phone, utility, and cable TV bills. Your credit report will also show every company that pulled your credit report within the past two years (called an "inquiry").

How long does information stay on my credit report? In theory, information stays on your credit report indefinitely. However, federal law—the Fair Credit Reporting Act (FCRA)—requires that any negative remarks be removed upon request after seven years (except for bankruptcy filing, which may remain for ten years). If you don't ask, however, negative information won't always go away.

How do I get negative information removed from my credit report? You may find some information on your report that is just plain wrong. Accounts that are not yours, judgments against people with similar names, and duplicate items are very common. Some items are more subtle, such as the fact that a debt is listed as still unpaid when in fact is was discharged in your bankruptcy. Ask the credit bureau in writing to reinvestigate the information. Under federal law, the bureau must reinvestigate and report back within 30 days. In some states, the law requires a shorter time period. If the bureau does not report back within the requisite time period, the item must be removed.

Communicating with Credit Bureaus

Send your letter by certified mail, return receipt requested. If you do not get results within the time period specified by your state law or the FCRA, you can write a sterner letter threatening to sue under state or federal law. You can also try to contact the creditor directly. Keep in mind that a creditor may also be liable for reporting wrong information. Before jumping into court, try contacting your regional Federal Trade Commission office and your state attorney general's Consumer Fraud Department.

Disputing Items on Your Credit Report

Do not be too specific with your request. For example, if a bureau reports that you had a judgment against you and it was paid, do not volunteer that information (a record of a judgment rendered and paid off is still worse than no judgment in the first place). Simply state that the information is incomplete and request that it be reinvestigated. In some cases, it is less work for the credit bureau to remove the item than to recheck it.

If you have "bad" items on your credit report, such as late payments, charge-offs, judgments, or a bankruptcy, the credit bureaus can legally report this information. However, if the information is stated in an incorrect or misleading format, you can still ask the bureaus to reinvestigate the information. Sometimes you will get lucky and the bureau does not report back within the required time period. In this event, the information must be removed.

What things affect my credit? Credit reports are based on a computer model, called a FICO score, developed by Fair Isaac and Co. (FICO, www.fairisaac.com). FICO scores range from 450–850. Typically the higher the FICO the higher LTV a lender will go, and the better rate they will offer you. Lenders change their FICO requirements on a monthly basis, and every lender has different requirements. Although the FICO formula is not generally known to the public, certain things tend to improve your score, such as the following:

- Installment loans (e.g., home mortgage, automobile) that are paid on time

- A few open credit lines with low balances

- A history of living at the same address

- Owning a home

Beyond the obvious late payments, judgments, and bankruptcy, there are certain subtle things that lower your score, such as the following:

- Too many revolving credit card accounts

- Too many inquiries

- High balances on credit cards

- Too many recently opened accounts

How can I improve my credit? A good credit score is generally above 660. Some loans are so stringent that they require a FICO score above 700. If your score is above 700, you have excellent credit. The bad news is, if you keep borrowing, your score will fall, even if you are current on all payments. So, in short, use your credit wisely. You can check your own FICO score at <www.myfico.com or www.freecreditreport.com>.

If you do not have late payments but want to improve your credit score, you should

- stay away from multiple department store cards—too many open accounts;

- bring a copy of your credit report when shopping for a loan— car dealers may run your credit a dozen times in one day of shopping, leaving damaging "inquiries."

- separate your credit file from your spouse's and remove each other's names from your credit cards; if you have authorization to use your spouse's card, it ends up on your credit file, too.

- Avoid high balances on credit cards. If you make a major purchase or go on a vacation, split up the charges between several credit cards.

- Don't close old credit cards accounts. Keep them open and use them every once in a while.

Can I get a loan with bad credit? Whether you can get a loan with poor credit depends on the type of loan. Unsecured loans, such as credit cards and bank signature loans, usually require a good credit history. Secured loans, such as home mortgages and car loans, are a bit more flexible. Lenders are more aggressive and will take larger risks when the loan is secured by collateral. The lender may require a larger down payment and charge a higher interest rate for the risk of lending to an individual with poor credit.

"I Don't Like Credit Cards—Should I Pay Them Off and Cancel Them?"

Never pay off completely or cancel a credit card! A person with no credit at all is worse off than a person with a bad credit history. You may think that credit cards are evil, but you may not be able to get a phone, a job, or even a utility account without a credit score. A person with an empty credit file looks somewhere between "suspicious" and "scary" to a company inquiring about your credit. Have a credit card or two, and use them once or twice a year, even if it is just to pay to fill up your gas tank.

If you carry debt on your credit card, don't carry more than 40 percent of the available credit at one time. Any more than this tends to lower your credit score. If need be, get two or more credit cards and split things up.

Your Provable Income

FNMA loan regulations require proof of requisite income to support the loan payments. Proof of income requires strict documentation, such as

- two years of W-2 forms,

- past two pay stubs, and

- two years of tax returns.

If you are self-employed, or at least a 25 percent owner of a business, you need to show that you have been in business at least two years. Proof of self-employment requires copies of tax returns showing the business income.

A good way to prove you are in business is to form a limited liability company (LLC). Lenders use secretary of state web sites to confirm the borrower's company has been registered more than two years. A lender may also ask for a letter from your accountant or CPA to verify that you have been in business for two years.

The Property

An understated point thus far is the property itself. Part of the lender's risk analysis is the property they are collateralizing with the loan. The lender has to keep in the back of its mind the worst-case scenario: a borrower's default and ensuing foreclosure. In other words, the lender asks itself, "Would I want to own this property?"

The appraisal. The first thing a lender will do is order an appraisal. Some lenders have in-house staff, but most use independent contractors. Because the appraiser charges his or her fee whether or not the loan is approved, the lender generally collects the appraisal fee (about $350) from the borrower up front.

Many lenders order a desk review and/or a field review of an appraisal as a way to check the quality of their appraisers. Therefore, one can assume that besides the underwriter and the appraiser, several other people have reviewed the appraisal. These costs are sometimes passed onto the borrower.

There are three generally accepted approaches to appraising property: the market data approach, the cost approach, and the income approach.

The Comparable Sales Approach. The comparable sales method is the most commonly used—and the most accurate one—to determine the value of single-family homes, condominiums, and small rental buildings (two to four units). Much of the legwork noted here is what a professional appraiser would do. (We've provided a sample appraisal report in Appendix D, beginning on page 187.)

When looking at comparables sales, an appraiser looks at actual sales, not listings. Remember, a listing price is an asking price. Novice investors often look at listing prices to determine what a house is worth, but this isn't as accurate as looking at properties that have sold in within the last 6 to 12 months. Listing prices become relevant, however, if they're substantially different than the sold prices because it indicates trends (for example, a rapidly appreciating or declining market).

Be careful using Web sites like "Zillow.com" that offer a computer-generated valuation. These are automated valuation models (AVMs), which are statistical models of many comparable sales of reportedly similar comparables. Many times they're not similar, but they're generally accurate within 10 percent if the houses in the area are very similar. It is less accurate in areas where there's a wide variety of homes, such as in an older neighborhood.

While many factors come into play in evaluating a residential property's value by comps, the three key factors are location, size of the home, and the number of bedrooms and bathrooms.

Location, location—A professional appraiser typically looks at houses in the same subdivision and so should you. In the case of a subdivision where the houses are all similar and built in the same time period, an appraiser need to compare similar houses with similar styles to get an accurate valuation. If there's a wide mix of properties in the subdivision, he may need to go outside of it to get comparable sales. Appraisers and loan underwriters generally look at comparables sales within one mile of the subject property. However, in populated cities, one mile may be too far. In rural areas, one mile may be too close.

Within a subdivision, there are many variations in lots that affect privacy, road noise, or sunlight. These lot variations won't affect the valuation unless an extreme difference exists. For example, if a row of houses backs to a major road, this may drop the value of the house as much as 10 percent. If a row of houses backs to power lines or a garbage dump, the discount may be even more substantial.

On the other hand, a great view may affect the lot substantially—in a positive way, of course. A location on a golf course, lake, ocean, or simply having a killer view may push values up by 25 percent or more.

Square footage. When determining a home's value, an appraiser will look to the home's square footage. Note that appraisers typically look at homes that are within 20 percent up or down in square footage as comparables.

Not all square footage is created equal. Most people think that if a house has 1,000 square feet and is worth $100,000, then the 1,100 square-foot house next door would be worth $110,000. Wrong. The extra 10 percent in square footage equals only a few percentage points in value. If these two houses offer the same location, style, and number of bedrooms and baths, the 10 percent additional square footage won't change the valuation much. Why? Because there is a fixed cost on a house based on the value of the land, cost of construction, sewer, subdivision plans, and more. An extra few hundred feet of space involves very little cost—only wood, nails, carpet, and possibly some minor electrical and plumbing costs.

Below-ground space. While finished basements can add value, the amount of value is less than it is for above-ground living areas. Plus, this greatly varies depending on different regions of the country. In humid areas, below-ground living space isn't as valuable to home-owners as in dryer areas of the country. Thus, the American National Standards Institute (ANSI) uses above-ground construction as the national standard for comparing values.

Sometimes homeowners refinish basements (or add other space) without obtaining proper building permits from the county. An appraiser may check public records to see if the finished square foot-age represented by the seller matches the county's file.

Bedrooms and baths. To determine a home's value using comps, an appraiser will also look at the quality and number of bedrooms and bathrooms. The most common bedroom-and-bathroom combinations:

- two bedrooms and one bathroom ("two-one"),

- two bedrooms and two bathrooms ("two-two"),

- three bedrooms and one bathroom ("three-one"), and

- three bedrooms and two bathrooms ("three-two").

A full bathroom includes a shower, bath, toilet, and sink. A half bath has a toilet and sink but no tub or shower.

The income approach. With income properties, an appraiser will also use the income approach method, particularly if comparable properties are not available for comparison. The income approach is basically a mathematical formula based on certain presumptions in the marketplace (based, of course, on opinion). The formula is as follows:

Value = Net operating income ÷ Capitalization rate

Net operating income is the potential (not actual) rents the prop-erty will command, less average vacancy allowance and operating expenses. Operating expenses include property management, insurance, property taxes, utilities, maintenance, and the like, but not mortgage loan payments.

Capitalization rate is a little more subjective and difficult to calculate. Capitalization, or "cap" rate, is the rate of return a particular investor would expect to receive if he or she purchased a similar property at a similar price. The cap rate is derived from looking at similar properties and the net operating income associated with them. Obviously, estimating cap rate is not an exact science but a trained guess.

Gross rent multiplier. For single-family rentals, duplexes, and other small projects, an appraiser may use the "gross rent multiplier" to help determine value. This formula basically looks at similar properties and their rental incomes. By dividing the sales prices of similar properties by the monthly rent received, the appraiser can come up with a rough formula to compare with the subject property.

Cap rates and other mathematical formulas are based solely on the property's income potential without regard to the financing. Obviously, the higher the debt payments on a property, the lower the cash flow. While these formulas can be used to compare properties side by side, keep in mind that the same financing may not be available. For example, a single family house may have a cap rate of 7 percent, but can be purchased with a small down payment. A nine-unit apartment building with a cap rate of 11 percent may require a 25 percent down payment, and interest rates available for financing could be 1 percent higher. The bottom line is that you must not look at mathematical formulas like cap rate in a vaccuum.

Replacement cost approach. Using this method of valuating a property, you add the value of the land, the age of the building, and the cost to reconstruct the building. It's important to go by today's costs, not original construction costs, because it would most likely be more expensive to construct the building at current prices. The goal is to figure out what it would cost today to replace the building if it were destroyed by a fire, natural disaster, or other unexpected event.

The cost replacement approach is not as accurate as comps because of the variations of land values. For example, a "shack" on the beach that can be replaced for a few hundred thousand does not take into account the value of the land.

Loan-to-Value

Loan-to-value (LTV) is an important criterion in determining the lender's risk. In maximizing leverage, the investor wants to invest as little cash as possible. However, the lender's point of view is that the more equity in the property, the less of a loss it would take if it had to foreclose.

Basic FNMA-conforming loan guidelines generally require an investor to put 20 percent cash down on a purchase, which means an 80 percent LTV. Nonconforming loans may permit as little as 0% down for investors, depending on the financial strength of the borrower. Thus, an investor with excellent credit and provable source of income may be able to borrow as much as 95 percent of the purchase price of an investment property. On the other hand, an investor with mediocre credit and who is self-employed for a short period of time may be required to put 20 percent down. There are a hundred variations, depending on the particular lender's underwriting criteria.

Loan-to-Value versus Loan-to-Purchase Price

Loan-to-value is determined by the amount of the loan compared to the appraised value of the property. If the investor is buying a property for less than the appraised value, then the lender's LTV criteria should change, correct? Actually, not—most lenders' LTV criteria are based on the appraised value or purchase price, whichever is less. Based on various studies done by lenders, the statistical chance of a borrower's default decreases if the borrower has more of his or her own money invested.

The Down Payment

You need to show at least two months of bank statements to the lender to prove that you have the requisite down payment on hand. If the down payment money suddenly "appeared" in your account, you need to show where it came from. If a borrower is putting up less than a 20 percent down payment, a lender may want to see that this money has been "seasoned," that is, is has been sitting in the borrower's bank account for a few months. The lender will request a VOD (verification of deposit) from the borrower's bank. If the money miraculously showed up in the borrower's bank account last week, the lender may get suspicious and want to know where it came from. Lenders generally don't like it when you borrow your down payment from someone else. If it was a gift, for example, from a relative, you'll need a letter from that relative stating so. Basically, the lender wants to make sure you didn't borrow the money for the down payment (although some lenders will permit you to borrow the down payment from your home equity line of credit, discussed in Chapter 6). If your credit report shows recently high balances or a lot of recent inquiries from credit card companies, this may be a red flag for the lender. In short, don't expect to borrow the down payment from a credit card or other unsecured line and think the lender won't notice.

Income Potential and Resale Value of the Property

The particular property being financed is relevant to the lender's risk. If the property is a single-family home in a "bread and butter" neighborhood, the lender's risk is reduced. Because middle-class homes in established neighborhoods are easy to sell, a lender feels secure using them as collateral. However, if the property is in a neighborhood where sales are not brisk, the lender's risk is increased. Also, if the property is very old or nonconforming with the neighborhood (e.g., one bedroom or very small), then the lender will be tighter with their underwriting guidelines. On the other hand, the stronger the local economy, the more likely a lender will be to waive the strictest of their loan guidelines.

Financing Junker Properties

One of the major headaches you will run into as an investor is trying to finance fixer-upper properties. Many banks shy away from these loans because a subpar property doesn't meet the strict FNMA lending guidelines. Also, lenders based their LTV and down payment requirements on the purchase price, not the appraisal. Thus, you are penalized as an investor for getting a good deal.

☞ **Example:** A property is worth $100,000 in good shape and needs $15,000 in repairs. The investor negotiates a purchase price of $70,000. The lender offers 80% LTV financing, which should be $80,000, right? Wrong! The lender offers 80% of the purchase price or appraised value, whichever is *less*. So, the lender would expect the borrower to come up with 20% of $70,000, or $14,000, offering $56,000 in financing.

Dealing with junker properties requires a lender that understands what it is you do. A small, locally owned bank that portfolios its loans will be your best bet. The lender may even lend you the fix-up money for the deal. An appraisal will be done of the property, noting its current value and its value after repairs are complete. The lender will lend you the money for the purchase, holding the repair money in escrow. When the repairs are completed, the lender will inspect the property, then authorize the release of the funds in escrow. If you pay for the property with your own cash and attempt to refinance it to get your money back, most lenders will only lend 75 to 80 percent of the after-repaired-value. This is consider a "cash out" refinance, that is, you are walking away with cash after the closing in your pocket.

If you have a loan on the property the lender will lend up to the amount of the existing loan, but few will lend more than 80 percent of the value of the property. Whenever you are paying off existing debt, the refinance loan is not considered "cash out."

Financing Trick

If you have an LLC or other corporate entity, you can lend the money to your company, then have your company lend it back to you, secured by a lien (mortgage or deed of trust) on the property. When you refinance the property, the loan is paid off to your company and thus is not technically a "cash out" refi. Some lenders may balk, however, if they realize that you are the owner of the company. Don't hide this fact from your lender, but don't volunteer it either.

Refinancing—Worth It?

A corollary to financing properties is the concept of refinancing. When and how often should you refinance your investment properties? Should you take advantage of falling interest rates?

The rule of thumb is that you should not refinance your loan unless it is a variable rate or your new rate is 2 percent lower than your existing rate (that is, 2 points lower—not 2 percent of your current rate—such as 8 percent down to 6 percent). However, this rule of thumb is just that—a guideline. There are costs involved in getting a loan, and it takes several years of payments at the lower rate to recoup your investment. Also, keep in mind that if your existing loan has been amortized for several years, you are starting to pay less interest and more principal on your current loan; refinancing means starting all over again.

Typically refinancing pays for itself within twenty-four to thirty-six months, depending on the loan costs. If you keep the property longer, refinancing makes sense and, vice-versa less time. The bottom line is to use common sense and a calculator—figure out whether the interest savings is worth the extra cost (and potentially the risk) of refinancing.

Filling Out a Loan Application

You should be familiar with FNMA Form 1003, a standard loan application form used by most mortgage brokers and direct lenders to gather information about your finances. You should also have one filled out on your computer that you can provide to your lender (you can download a fillable Form 1003 from <www.legalwiz.com/1003.htm>. You should always fill out a Form 1003 truthfully and honestly, but, like income tax returns, there are many "gray areas" when it comes to stating your income, debt, and assets. If you have any doubt, have your mortgage broker review it before submitting it to the lender.

Cash Out Refinancing

Many investors refinance every few years as property values increase, using the extra cash to buy more properties, as suggested in Robert Allen's best-selling book, *Nothing Down for the '90s*. While this process does increase your leverage, it also increases your risk. There is nothing inherently wrong with taking out cash in a refinance, so long as the cash is used wisely. Spending the money as profit is not a smart use. Paying off credit cards with that money isn't always a smart use of cash either because you are taking unsecured debt and substituting it with secured debt. While it may seem like the monthly payments are lower, the expense of the refinance hardly makes it worthwhile. And if you end up with a high LTV and/or negative cash flow on the property and housing prices fall, you are in for a world of financial hurt.

Key Points

- Lenders make their profit in a variety of ways—the key is understanding how they do it, and paying the minimum you need to get a good loan at a fair price.

- Choose a mortgage company that has the requisite experience and can handle your business.

- Understand the basic loan criteria before you apply for a loan.

- Refinance only when the numbers make sense.

CHAPTER 5

Creative Financing through Institutional Lenders

The power of thought—the magic of the mind!

—Lord Byron

While having a good mortgage broker or lender on your side is very valuable, you still need to have a few tricks in your back pocket to make things work. One of the main challenges for the investor is to buy properties with little or no cash, yet still have a low enough payment to avoid negative cash flow. This chapter will discuss some of the ways to do so.

Double Closing—Short-Term Financing without Cash

If your intention is to buy a property and turn it around quickly for a cash profit, it is almost a sin to pay loan costs. Known as a *flip,* the investor wants to make $5,000 to $10,000 turning a property that he or she buys at a bargain price. This process can be accomplished without traditional bank financing, much less a down payment.

If a particular seller and buyer cannot be present at the same time, a closing can be consummated *in escrow* (an incomplete transaction, waiting for certain conditions to be met, such as the funding of a loan). Thus, the seller can sign a deed and place it into escrow with the closing agent. When the buyer completes his or her loan transaction, the deed is delivered and the funds are disbursed. In many cases, you can buy and sell the property to a third party in a back-to-back *double closing* (also called *double escrow* in some states). You do not need any of your own cash to purchase the property from the owner before reselling it to another investor/buyer in a double closing.

The seven-step double-closing process works as follows:

1. Party A signs a purchase agreement with party B at a below-market price.

2. Party B signs a purchase agreement with party C, offering the property at market price.

3. The only party coming to the table with cash is party C. Assuming party C is borrowing money from a lender to fund the transaction, party C's bank will wire the funds into the bank account of the closing agent.

4. Party A signs a deed to party B. This deed is *not delivered* but deposited in escrow with the closing agent. Party B signs a deed to party C, which is deposited in escrow with the closing agent.

5. Party C signs the bank loan documents, at which point the loan is funded and the transaction is complete.

6. The closing agent delivers funds to party A for the purchase price and the difference to party B.

7. The closing agent records the two deeds one after another at the county land records office.

As you can see, no cash was required by party B to close the transaction. Party B's funds came from the proceeds of the sale from party B to party C. If the second sale does not happen, the first transaction, which is closed in escrow, cannot be completed. At that point, the deal is dead.

If you are doing a double closing, you are acting as both buyer and seller. A double closing is actually two separate transactions. If you do not want party C to meet party A, the double closing can be completed in two phases rather than all at once. Obviously, you cannot give the seller funds until your buyer gives you funds. Thus, one of the two transactions must be closed in escrow until the other is complete. Often, this escrow closing may last an hour. The bottom line is you cannot close with the owner if your third-party buyer does not deliver funds to you.

If you are interested in more information about the flipping process, pick up a copy of my book, *Flipping Properties* (Kaplan Publishing, 2007).

Seasoning of Title

In recent years, some lenders have been placing "seasoning" (time of ownership) requirements on loan transactions. Some lenders are afraid to fund the second part of a double closing because of the possibility that the buyer's purchase price is inflated. The lenders are acting mostly out of irrational fear because of a recent barrage of real estate scams reported in the newspapers.

Property flipping scams. There has been a lot of negative press lately about double closings. Scores of people have been indicted under what the press has called "property flipping schemes." Some lenders, real estate agents, and title companies will tell you that double closings are illegal. In fact, they are nothing of the sort.

The illegal property-flipping schemes work as follows. Unscrupulous investors buy cheap, run-down properties in mostly low-income neighborhoods. After they do shoddy renovations to the properties, they sell them to unsophisticated buyers at an inflated price. In most cases, the investor, appraiser, and mortgage broker conspire by submitting fraudulent loan documents and a bogus appraisal. The end result is a buyer who has paid too much for a house and cannot afford the loan. Because many of these loans are FHA-insured, the U.S. Senate has held hearings to investigate this practice.

Despite the negative press, neither flipping nor double closings are illegal. The activities described above simply amount to loan fraud, nothing more. As a result, some lenders have placed seasoning requirements on the seller's ownership. If the seller has not owned the property for at least 12 months, the lender will assume that the deal is fishy and refuse to fund the buyer's loan. There really is no solution to this issue other than to deal with other lenders that don't have the seasoning hangup. Make sure you stay in control of the loan process and offer a recommendation of mortgage company that doesn't have a problem with double closings.

Two possible solutions. If the buyer has found a lender that is really stuck on the seasoning issue, you have two options: (1) assign your contract to the end-buyer or (2) have the original owner buy you out of the deal.

If you assign your contract to your end-buyer, he or she will close directly with the owner. However, the end-buyer may not have enough cash to pay you the difference between your purchase price with the owner and his or her purchase price with you. You need to trust that the parties involved will pay you at closing from the seller's proceeds!

The safer way to solve the problem is to approach the owner and ask him or her to buy you out of the deal. *Buying you out* means that the owner is going to pay you to cancel the sales agreement with you so that he or she can enter into a purchase contract directly with your end-buyer. Ideally, it would be best if the owner paid you in cash before he or she closed with your end-buyer. If the owner wants to wait until the end-buyer closes the sale with him or her to pay you the cash, put the agreement in writing in the form of a promissory note, secured by a mortgage on the property. Thus, at closing, you will be paid off as a lien holder.

This "workaround" should only be used in limited circumstances since it almost looks like you are a real estate broker. If you make a wholesale operation of the process, you will likely get the attention of your state's real estate licensing agency.

The Middleman Technique

Many foolish investors and unscrupulous mortgage brokers have been known to "overappraise" a property, effectively financing a property for 100 percent of its value. The mortgage broker then passes the buyer's down payment back to the buyer under the table so that the deal is done with nothing down. Not only is this practice illegal, it is foolish, unless the property can be rented for more than the loan payment.

Again, there is nothing special about buying a property with no money down unless it is profitable to do so. If you can purchase the property at a substantially below-market price *and* with no money down, you then have a good deal. This is buying 100 percent loan-to-purchase, not 100 percent loan to value.

The problem with buying a property at a below-market price is that conventional lenders tend to penalize you with their loan regulations. As discussed earlier, FNMA-conforming loan guidelines usually require that an investor put up 20 percent of his or her own cash as a down payment. The 20 percent rule applies even if the purchase price is half of the property's appraised value. A common, but illegal, practice is for the buyer to put up the down payment and for the seller to give it back to the buyer after closing. People may get away with it all the time, but this practice is loan fraud.

The middleman technique is a legal way to get around the 20 percent down rule. The process requires the following three important factors:

1. A middleman buyer

2. A negotiated purchase price that is 10 percent to 20 percent below market value

3. A lender that does not require evidence of a cash down payment

Use a middleman partner to buy the house from the owner at a discount and sell it to you for its full appraised value. Do a double closing at which time the middleman buys the property and simultaneously sells to you. The reason for the middleman buyer is to increase the purchase price, because most lenders base their LTV on the lesser of the purchase price or the appraised value. Thus, even if you negotiate a 20 percent discount in the purchase price, the maximum loan you can get is based on the purchase price, not the appraised value.

☞ **Example:** Sammy Seller has a property worth $100,000 and is willing to accept $80,000 for an all-cash sale. Matthew Middleman signs a purchase contract to buy it from Sammy for $80,000. Matthew Middleman then signs a contract to sell the same property to Ira Investor for $100,000. The terms of the contract are $80,000 cash and a note for $20,000, due in ten years. Ira applies for a loan with First National Bank for 80 percent of the purchase price, or $80,000. At a double closing, Sammy signs a deed to Matthew, which is held in escrow. Matthew signs a deed to Ira, which is also held in escrow. First National Bank funds the loan by wiring the money into the account of the escrow agent. The closing agent writes Sammy a check for $80,000. Ira signs a note to Matthew for $20,000. The closing agent records the two deeds back-to-back. Sammy gets his $80,000. Ira gets his property for only a few thousand dollars down (his loan costs). Matthew gets a note from Ira for $20,000. See Figure 5.1.

Epilogue: A month or two after closing, Matthew and Ira become partners when Ira deeds a one-half interest in the property to Matthew in exchange for complete satisfaction of the note.

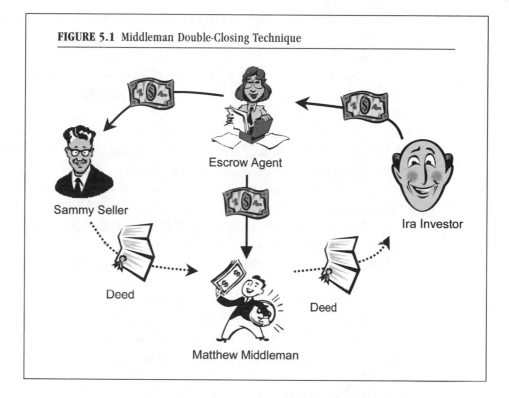

FIGURE 5.1 Middleman Double-Closing Technique

Escrow Agent

Sammy Seller

Ira Investor

Deed

Matthew Middleman

Deed

Warning: Keep in mind that you should disclose to the lender up front that you are not putting up any cash in the deal. Do not, I repeat, do not pay the seller cash at closing and take it back under the table in exchange for a note. This practice is loan fraud, punishable by up to 30 years in federal prison. *See 18 U.S.C. Sec. 1014.*

Case Study #1: Tag Team Investing

I stumbled across a property that was bank-owned and offered by auction to the public. Like many foreclosures, the property was in need of repair (approximately $10,000 worth, in this case). The market value of the property in its existing condition was about $180,000. The bank was willing to accept a bid of $134,000, which was 74 percent of its value.

I brought in a middleman to submit the bid of $134,000 to the bank. The terms of the offer were all cash, which the lender would receive, as explained in a moment.

The middleman then signed a contract to sell the property to me for $180,000. The terms of the sale from the middleman to me were $9,000 cash and a $27,000 promissory note (no payments, interest only, due in five years). The $27,000 note was to be secured by a second mortgage on the property, because I intended to borrow 80 percent of the purchase price ($144,000) and secure the new loan with a new first mortgage on the property.

After the double closing, I owned the property subject to a new first mortgage of $144,000 to an institutional lender and a second mortgage of $27,000 to the middleman investor. The bank that owned the property received their $134,000 in cash, and the middleman investor walked away with about $9,000 in cash. I was out of pocket about $11,000, which was the down payment ($9,000), plus closing costs ($2,000).

I later sold the property for $185,000, at which time the middleman investor agreed to accept a 50 percent discount on the $27,000 note. I used proceeds from the sale to pay the middleman. In the meantime, the payments on the $144,000 first mortgage note were less than I was able to rent the property for.

Case Study #2: Tag Team Investing

A client of ours (we'll call him Chuck) used the middleman method to buy a $1.6 million house with no money down. The property was banked-owned as the result of a foreclosure. Chuck set up a simple living trust for himself with his buddy as trustee. The trust signed a contract (executed by Chuck's buddy, the trustee) to buy the house from the bank for $950,000. Chuck then signed a contract to buy the house from the trust for $1.6 million, the property's appraised value. Chuck gave the trust $400,000 cash and borrowed $1.2 million from an institutional lender. Because Chuck was the beneficiary of the trust, he received the proceeds of the sale (his $400,000 down payment, plus the $250,000 loan proceeds), netting nearly $250,000 cash in his pocket. Needless to say, he has yet to reach into his pocket for a monthly payment on his new loan!

Walk the Fine Line Carefully

In Chuck's example, the lender never asked (nor did Chuck misrepresent) the relationship between the trust and himself. However, if the lender does ask about the relationship between you and the middleman, be truthful. Don't mislead or misrepresent anything to the lender you are borrowing from. It's one thing to be creative with a lender; it's another thing to lie.

Using Two Mortgages

In the Case Studies above, we got around the 20 percent down payment financing requirement by using a seller-carryback loan (discussed in more detail in Chapter 9). This type of loan is known as an 80-15-5 loan; you borrow a first mortgage loan for 80 percent of the purchase price, ask the seller to accept a note for 15 percent of the purchase price, and put down the balance of 5 percent in cash. There are many variations to this formula, such as 80-10-10 (80 percent first mortgage, 10 percent second mortgage, 10 percent down).

In Case Study #2, the seller accepted a note and second mortgage for part of the purchase price. The 10 percent (or more) can also be borrowed from a third party, such as an institutional lender. The advantage of using two loans as opposed to one 90 percent or 95 percent LTV loan, is that the underwriting requirements are easier on the 80 percent LTV first mortgage loan (and you avoid the PMI requirement, discussed in Chapter 3). Generally speaking, nonconforming lenders aren't as concerned with the source of the down payment or whether the borrower offers cash or a note (or other financing) for the balance of the purchase price. So long as the primary lender is in a first mortgage lien position at 80 percent LTV or less, they are fine with the seller accepting a note or the borrower obtaining some of the difference in the form of a second mortgage loan.

Tax Consequences to the Middleman

You may be wondering, "If the middleman sells the property to you at a profit, isn't this taxable income?" Yes and no. Although it looks like a profit is made, there is no real gain. The middleman, in Chuck's case, was a trust of which Chuck was the taxable owner, so there was no gain. In Case Study #1, the middleman's profit was a note, which is an installment sale. Installment sale income is taxed when the gain is actually received, not when the note is executed. In that particular case, no gain was received until the note was paid in full (in my case, it was only paid 50 percent, which was taxable income to the middleman).

No Documentation and Nonincome Verification Loans

Conforming loans generally require strict proof of income, assets, and other debts. If, for example, you cannot prove income to a lender, whether it is because you are self-employed for a short time or can't otherwise prove income, there are nonincome verification (NIV) loans.

NIV loans (also known as "stated income" loans) require less documentation than traditional loans. Lenders often advertise these programs as "no doc" loans, meaning the borrower does not have to come up with any documentation other than a credit report and a loan application.

Get Out the Calculator

Using a first and second mortgage in lieu of one larger loan may not make sense until you do the numbers. Surely, a second mortgage loan as described here will carry a higher interest rate because of the lender's increased risk of being in second position. Make sure the "blended" interest rate between the first and second mortgages does not exceed what you otherwise would be paying with a larger, single first mortgage loan. Also, keep in mind that a larger first mortgage loan may also mean you are paying private mortgage insurance, so that must be factored into the monthly payment.

How to Calculate a Blended Interest Rate

Multiply each interest rate times the amount it relates to the total debt, then add them together. For example, if you have an $80,000 first mortgage loan at 8%, and a $20,000 second mortgage loan at 10%, the blended rate is (8% × .8) + (10% × .2) = 8.4%.

Some loans are called "no ratio" loans, in that you don't have to justify your total debt (mortgages plus other continuing obligations, such as car loans and student loans) compared to your income.

Few, if any loans are true "no documentation" loans. Most of these offered programs are bait and switch tactics: The lender says they don't need documentation, but when the loan is being processed, the lender will ask for more and more documentation. Often, the lender will see some red flags that trigger the additional inquiry.

The best defense to these tactics is a good offense; speak to your lender or mortgage broker up front. Identify documentation issues up front, educate the lender about your finances, and be truthful. The more a lender suspects you are hiding something, the more documentation the lender will ask for.

Here is a real-world example: Carteret Mortgage, <www.nva-mortgage.com>, lists the following general guidelines for one of its no-ratio mortgage loans:

- Minimum middle credit score must be 640.

- Five credit accounts are required; three may be from alternative sources—utility, auto insurance, etc.

- Bankruptcy and foreclosures must be discharged for three years with reestablished credit.

- Two years' employment with same employer.

- Two months' PITI reserves are required with an LTV less than 80 percent. Six months' reserves are required otherwise.

- 10 percent minimum down payment is required from your own funds. No gifts.

You should ask for this kind of information up front from your mortgage broker or lender. The more information you know about what a lender needs, the more information you can provide.

Watch What You Say on NIV Loans

Just because you don't have to provide documentation of your income to the lender, it doesn't mean you have a license to lie. Most lenders will make you sign a Form 4506, an authorization to release federal income tax returns for the past 4 years. They may not check now, but if your loan goes into default, they may obtain copies of your tax returns. If the income you report on your loan application is way out of sync with your tax returns, you may be answering to loan fraud charges.

Develop a Loan Package

You should present a loan package of your own to any new lender. This package should include the following:

- Your completed FNMA Form 1003 loan application (See Appendix C.)

- A recent copy of your credit report, with written explanations of negative information

- A copy of the purchase contract for the subject property

- A copy of the down payment check and documented proof of where it came from

- Copies of recent tax returns, pay stubs, and W-2s (if applicable)

- Recent appraisal of the property if you have one, or a market analysis prepared by a real estate agent

- Copies of existing leases or information of rental value of similar properties

- Copies of recent bank statements, retirement plan accounts, and brokerage accounts

- Any other relevant financial information concerning assets or liabilities.

- Copy of title commitment and chain of title.

- CPA letter for self-employed borrowers.

The more information you provide up front, the fewer surprises the lender runs into, and hence the less likely it will be suspicious and ask for more documentation.

Subordination and Substitution of Collateral

Subordination is asking someone who holds a mortgage (or deed of trust) on your property to agree to make his or her lien *subordinate,* or second in line, to another lien. For example, suppose you own a property worth $100,000 that has a first mortgage to ABC Savings Bank for $65,000. If you want to borrow $30,000 from First National Bank secured by a second mortgage, you would have to pay a much higher interest rate because First National's mortgage would be subordinate, or second, to the lien in favor of ABC Savings Bank. See Figure 5.2. A second lien position is riskier than a first lien position, so the interest rate is generally higher to compensate the lender for its increased risk. If you could convince ABC Savings Bank to move its lien to second position, First National would now be a first mortgage holder and thus give you a better interest rate.

Keep in mind that you can use subordination to draw cash on properties you already own. If you purchased a property with seller financing, simply ask the former owner to subordinate his or her mortgage to a new first. This may require you to give the seller some incentive, such as additional cash or paydown of the principal. Either way, subordination is an excellent way to finance a purchase or draw money out of existing properties.

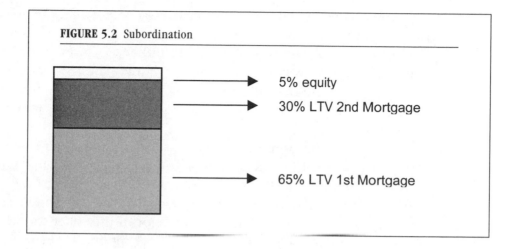

FIGURE 5.2 Subordination

5% equity

30% LTV 2nd Mortgage

65% LTV 1st Mortgage

Substitution of collateral is a method of moving a lien from one property, or collateral, to another. The substituted property does not necessarily have to be real estate. You can use a car or boat title as the substitute collateral. Better yet, get the mortgage holder to release the mortgage with no substitute collateral! To get someone to take a note without collateral, you need to offer a substantial cash down payment. Think about this: If the note you give the seller is not secured by the property, you can refinance or sell the real estate without paying off the note.

Case Study: Subordination and Substitution

A property owner (we'll call her Mrs. Seller) called me to discuss selling her house. After some negotiations, we agreed to purchase the property for $63,000 as follows:

- $35,000 cash at closing of title

- Promissory note and second mortgage (subordinate to a new first) for $28,000, payable in installments of $350 per month, no interest

She owned the house free and clear, so why would she do such a thing? The answer is, to have her needs met. After some discussion, she told me that she was sick of the upkeep of the property and wanted a brand-new doublewide mobile home. The $35,000 cash was for the new home, and the $350 per month would pay her mobile home lot rent (just so you know that I didn't "steal" the property from some little old lady!).

I went to a hard-money lender (discussed in Chapter 6) and borrowed $37,500 at 12 percent interest (only $35,000 went to the seller; the extra cash was for the points on the loan). I closed escrow, placing a new first mortgage in favor of the hard-money lender, and a second mortgage (subordinate to the first) in favor of the seller for $28,000. My total monthly payments were $725 per month, and I rented the property to a nice family for $800 per month.

A few years later, I wanted to sell the property, so I called Mrs. Seller and asked if she would be willing to take a discount on the amount we still owed her, which was approximately $20,000 (remember the original amount was $28,000). She said that she liked the monthly payments and didn't want me to pay her off! With that, she agreed to accept $10,000, release the mortgage from the property, and allow us to continue making payments on the $10,000 balance of the unsecured promissory note. Not only did we profit from the sale of the property, we also walked away from closing with an extra $10,000 cash in our pockets! The extra cash was due to the fact that we only paid her $10,000 towards the balance of the $20,000 debt still remaining. We continued to make monthly payments on the note, but because the security (mortgage) was released from the property, we received the cash from the proceeds of the sale.

As you can see, subordination and substitution of collateral are two powerful tools to make you more money in real estate.

> ### Zero-Interest Financing: The Exception to the "Cash Flow Is King" Rule
>
> In Mrs. Seller's case, the payments on the high-interest-rate first mortgage plus the owner-carry second mortgage were only slightly less than the market rent for the property. However, because the payments on the owner-carry second were for zero interest, the equity pay-down far exceeded the value of the cash flow. Zero-interest financing is one of the rare instances where monthly cash flow is not the investor's first concern.

Using Additional Collateral

If the lender you are dealing with feels uncomfortable with the collateral or your LTV requirements, offer additional security for the loan. There are several ways to securitize a loan, other than with a lien on the subject property.

Blanket Mortgage

A blanket mortgage is a lien that covers multiple properties. Developers often use a blanket mortgage that covers several lots. When each lot is developed and sold, the lien is released from that lot. A blanket mortgage (or deed of trust) is just like a regular lien, except that it names several properties as collateral. When recorded in county records, the lien is now placed on each property named in the security instrument. See Figure 5.3.

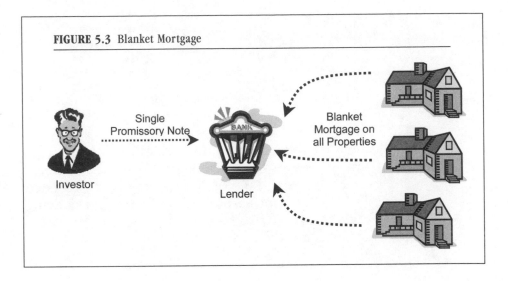

FIGURE 5.3 Blanket Mortgage

If you have other property with equity, even raw land, you can offer this property as additional security for the loan. Be cautious, however, with offering your personal residence as security; failure to make payments can make you homeless!

Using Bonds as Additional Collateral

A bond, like a note, is a debt instrument. In return for the loan, the investor is paid in full at a future date. Bonds generally pay interest at fixed periods, unless they are zero-coupon bonds. The cash value of a bond at any given time is based on the maturity date and its present value, which in turn is based on whether investors are speculating interest rates will rise or fall in the future. As interest rates fall, bond prices rise, and vice versa. And, logically, the later the maturity date, the less the present value of the bond.

Municipal and government bonds are virtually the same as cash; they can be traded, sold, and hypothecated (used as collateral). U.S. Treasury bonds are safe, secure investments from a risk standpoint.

From an investment standpoint, they are a fair to good bet, depending on interest rates and market inflation.

Most laypeople think of bonds as being a secure investment. Of course, institutional lenders are generally too savvy to accept the face value of a bond as collateral. However, when dealing with a private motivated seller, an owner-carry offer that is cross-collateralized with U.S. Treasury bonds sounds appealing. When making an offer to a seller with owner financing, offer the face value of the bond as collateral. Although the present value may be less, the very idea of a bond as additional collateral sounds safe. Furthermore, bonds can be used in lieu of a down payment.

Example: Sonny Seller owns a house free and clear and is asking $100,000 for his house. Brian Buyer offers Sonny $110,000 as follows: $30,000 in U.S. Treasury bonds and an $80,000 note secured by a mortgage on the property. The $30,000 in bonds, if they matured in 30 years, can be bought for a fraction of their face value, depending on the market interest rates. In the seller's mind, he's receiving more than the asking price, but the buyer is paying much less than the asking price (sometimes sellers are stuck on asking price just because they are ashamed to tell their neighbors they took less!).

For an excellent reference on using bonds as collateral for real estate financing, I recommend *Formulas for Wealth* by Richard Powelson, Ph.D. (Skyward Publishing, 2001). For more information on bonds, try <www.savingsbonds.gov>.

Key Points

- Avoid loan costs on flips—use the double closing.

- Use the middleman technique to overcome lender down payment requirements.

- Don't let lack of income hold you back—use NIV loans.

- Think beyond the property for collateral: substitute, subordinate, and cross-collateralize.

CHAPTER 6

Hard Money and Private Money

A loan shark is simply a thief without a Wall Street office.

—Lyndon H. LaRouche Jr.

An often overlooked and very valuable source of funding is private money. Small companies and individual investors called "hard-money lenders" are an excellent resource for quick cash. Private lenders are often known as hard-money lenders because they charge very high interest rates. Hard money is often called "bridge" or "mezzanine" financing, which is more palatable. I have personally borrowed at 18 percent with 8 points as an origination fee! These rates may sound outrageous at first blush, but it is the availability of the money not the cost that matters.

Emergency Money

I recently won with the high bid on a condominium auctioned by the Department of Veterans Affairs (VA). I made the bid in the name of a corporation rather than my individual name. I was assured by my mortgage broker that the lender that had my loan application would permit me to finance the purchase in a corporation. At the eleventh hour, the lender changed its mind, requiring me to close in my individual name. I asked the VA for permission to amend the purchase contract to name me, rather than my corporation. The VA refused, and I now had less than five days to close or lose the deal. Because my winning purchase bid was an excellent price, I opted for using hard money to purchase the property. I paid 14 percent interest for a few months, then refinanced the property at a good interest rate. All in all, the high cost of the hard-money loan was worth it and saved me in a pinch.

Hard-money lending criteria are based on the collateral (the property) rather than the financial strength of the borrower. For this reason, hard-money lenders are often referred to as "equity" lenders. A hard-money lender looks at a loan, thinking, "Would I want to own this property for the amount of money I lend this person?" Hard-money lenders generally go no higher than a 75 percent loan-to-value. The goods news, however, is that many hard-money lenders will base their loan on appraised value, not purchase price. So, if you negotiate a very good purchase price, you may end up with an 85 percent loan-to-purchase ratio.

Hard-money lenders can be expensive but also easy to deal with if you are in a hurry for the money. In many cases, the availability of the money is more important than the cost of borrowing it.

Where to Find Hard-Money Lenders

Hard-money lenders are fairly easy to find, once you know where to look. The first place is your local newspaper, under "money to loan." The ads will usually look something like this:

**Stop Foreclosure! Real Estate Loans.
Fast and Easy. No Credit Required.
48-Hour Funding. Call Fred 555-1134.**

Many hard-money lenders advertise on the Internet. Try a Yahoo! search of the Internet for hard-money lender Web sites. Not all hard-money lenders call themselves that; some use the title "equity-based lender." It is best to find one that is located within your state. A referral from another local real estate investor is helpful, too. For a referral to a local real estate investors club in your city, try the National Real Estate Investors Association at <www.nationalreia.com>.

Borrowing from Friends and Relatives

Friends and relatives seem like obvious choices for borrowing money, but they may be as skeptical as an institutional lender. They may try to boss you around and nag you about when you expect to repay the money you borrowed. They may also want to be part of the daily decision-making process, which would interfere with your business. And, of course, they may be emotional about their money, whereas institutional lenders don't take money matters personally.

Borrower Beware! Soliciting money from private investors can be a dangerous practice. Federal securities laws may apply to public solicitations of money as a "public offering." In addition, state securities regulations (known as "Blue Sky Laws") may also apply. Simply running a blind ad in the paper stating, "Private Money Wanted for Real Estate Purchase—12% Return" may result in a call from your state attorney general's office. If you are approaching a friend, relative, or individual investor to borrow money secured by a specific property, then you are probably OK; borrowing money for a "pool" of funds becomes trickier. Also, when you deal with strangers, multiple parties, or the public at large, you should seek the advice of a local attorney knowledgeable about state and federal securities regulations.

Using Lines of Credit

A home equity line of credit (HELOC) can be an excellent financing tool, if it is used properly. A HELOC is basically like a credit card secured by a mortgage or deed of trust on your property. In most cases, it will be a second lien. You only pay interest on the amounts you borrow on the HELOC. You can access the HELOC by writing checks provided by the lender.

HELOCs are being advertised on television as a way to consolidate debt, but they can be used much more effectively by investors. When you need cash in a hurry for a short period of time, a HELOC can be very useful. For example, if a seller tells you to give him "$75,000 cash on Friday and I'll sell you my house for a song," you need to act in a hurry. Another example of cash in a hurry is a foreclosure auction, which, in many states, requires payment at the end of the day of the auction. When you need cash in a hurry, there's no time to go to the bank.

Deducting HELOC Interest

There are limits on the deductions you can take on your personal tax return for interest paid on your HELOC. Generally speaking, you can only deduct that portion of interest on debt that does not exceed the value of your home and is less than $100,000. But, if you do your real estate investments as a corporate entity, you can always loan the money to that entity and have the entity take the deduction as a business interest expense. This transaction must, of course, be reported on your personal return and must be an "arms-length" transaction (i.e., documented in writing and within the realm of a normal business transaction). Consult with your tax advisor before proceeding with this strategy.

While the HELOC may be a high-interest-rate loan, it is a temporary financing source that can be repaid when you refinance the property. *Do not use your HELOC as a permanent down payment or any other long-term financing source—it will generally get you into financial trouble.* Furthermore, some institutional lenders may not lend you the balance if you borrowed the funds for the down payment. Other lenders allow you to borrow the money from your HELOC, but count the borrowed money against your debt-to-income ratio. You also need to count this debt against any property you purchase to determine cash flow.

Warning: Failure to pay your HELOC means you lose your home! Use your HELOC wisely and only if it means losing a steal of a deal if you don't!

Credit Cards

You may already have more available credit than you realize. Credit cards and other existing revolving debt accounts can be quite useful in real estate investing. Most major credit cards allow you to take cash advances or write checks to borrow on the account. The transaction fees and interest rates are fairly high, but you can access this money on 24 hours' notice. Also, because credit card loans are unsecured, there are no other loan costs normally associated with a real estate transaction, such as title insurance, appraisals, pest inspections, surveys, etc.

Often, you will be better off paying 18 percent interest or more on a credit line for three to six months than paying 9 percent interest on institutional loans that have up-front costs that would take you years to recoup. Again, use credit cards carefully and only as a temporary solution if the deal calls for it.

Key Points

- Hard money is an excellent short-term financing tool.

- HELOCs and credit cards are excellent sources for fast cash.

CHAPTER 7

Partnerships and Equity Sharing

The guy with the experience approaches the guy with the money. When the deal is complete, the guy with the experience has the money, and the guy who had the money has experience.

–Anonymous

If you are low on cash or have cash and are low on time, a partnership or equity-sharing arrangement may be for you. Using partners to finance real estate transactions is the classic form of using other people's money (OPM). Experienced investors are always willing to put up money to be a partner in a profitable real estate transaction. As with many businesses, talent is more important than cash. If you can find a good real estate deal, the money will often find its way to you!

Partnership arrangements work in a variety of circumstances. The most common scenario involves one party living in the property while the other does not. Another scenario may involve all of the parties living in the property. These arrangements are common among family members. Parents often lend their children money for a down payment on a house, with a promise of repayment at a later date.

101

If the repayment of the debt is with interest and/or relates to the future appreciation of the property, we have a basic equity-sharing arrangement.

Another common financing arrangement between multiple parties is a partnership wherein none of the parties live in the property. This chapter will discuss the basic partnership investment. Larger investments through limited partnerships and other corporate entities in a "pool" of money are known as "syndications." These investments are generally classified as securities, so compliance with state and federal regulations is complex. Thus, syndications are generally not recommended for financing smaller projects because the legal fees for compliance with securities laws will far exceed the benefit of raising capital through multiple investors.

Basic Equity-Sharing Arrangement

The common equity-sharing arrangement involves one party living in the property and the other putting up cash and/or financing. Both the occupant and the nonoccupant enjoy tax benefits and share the profit, as described later in this chapter. First-time homebuyers make the best resident partners while family members, sellers, and real estate investors fill the nonresident partner role.

Scenario #1: Buyer with Credit and No Cash

A lot of potential homebuyers have the income to qualify for a mortgage loan, but only with a substantial down payment. With a small down payment, the monthly loan payments may be too high. A potential homebuyer could borrow the money for the down payment, but nobody but a fool (or a parent) would lend $25,000 or more unsecured. Furthermore, loan regulations generally do not permit the use of borrowed money as a down payment.

An equity-sharing partner could put up the money in exchange for an interest in the property. The resident partner would obtain the loan, live in the property, make the monthly loan payments, and maintain the property. The nonresident partner who puts up the down-payment money is free from management headaches and negative cash flow. After a number of years (typically five to seven), the property is sold, the mortgage loan balance is paid in full, and the profits are split between the parties. Obviously, the strategy works best in a rising real estate market.

Scenario #2: Buyer with Cash and No Credit

The second equity-sharing scenario would be a buyer with cash but an inability to qualify for institutional financing. The resident partner would put up the down payment, the nonresident partner would obtain the loan. After a number of years, the property is sold, the mortgage loan balance is paid in full, and the profits are split between the parties.

Your Credit Is Worth More Than Cash

Just because you put up credit and no cash does not mean you aren't at risk. Cash is easy to come by, but good credit takes years to build, and only months to ruin. As I write this book, an investor friend of mine (we'll call him Brian) recalls his first deal. Brian was a neophyte investor who was approached by an experienced investor with the following proposal: "You put up your credit to get the loan; I'll put up the cash for the down payment." Brian bought the property with the investor in this manner, but Brian did not manage the property. Brian received a call from the lender a year later and was informed that the mortgage loan had not been paid in several months. Brian was unable to locate his partner who had apparently collected the rents and skipped town.

The moral of this story: Use your credit wisely—cash can be recouped in a few months, but credit blemishes can take years to fix.

Tax Code Compliance

Equity-sharing arrangements are governed by Section 280A of the Internal Revenue Code (IRC). Labeled a Shared Equity Financing Agreement (SEFA), IRC Section 280A permits the nonresident partner investment property tax benefits (namely depreciation). In addition, the resident partner can take advantage of the benefits of owning a principal residence (namely, the mortgage interest deduction).

The nonresident partner is essentially treated for tax purposes as a landlord, taking depreciation for his or her ownership interest to the extent he or she receives rent. So, for example, if fair market rent for the property is $1,000 per month and the resident/nonresident equity split is 60/40, then the resident must pay $400 in rent to the nonresident partner if the nonresident wants to take the depreciation deduction. In turn, the nonresident partner returns the rent to property expenses for which the resident partner is responsible (in this way, the cash contribution by the resident partner is not increased—it is just shifted to conform with the tax code). If the resident does not pay rent, but rather makes all of the mortgage interest payments directly to the lender, then the investor receives no tax benefits, leaving them all to the resident. The agreement can be made in a number of ways, depending on the needs of the parties and their needs for the tax deductions.

The parties must have a co-ownership agreement that complies with IRC Section 280A in order to reap the benefits of this mixed use tax plan. If the relationship is deemed a "partnership" by the IRS, then the rules of IRC Section 280A are not applicable. A highly recommended book that covers the tax implication in detail is *The New Home Buying Strategy* by Marilyn Sullivan, Esq., <www.msullivan.com>.

Depreciation Is Often an Overrated Deduction

With breakeven or even slightly positive cash flow, the deprecation deduction creates a "paper loss" for the investor. The loss can be used to offset the investor's other income. Keep two things in mind. First, the deduction is not always available to the investor, depending on his other income. Second, the depreciation taken on a rental property is recaptured (realized as a gain) when the property is sold. In short, don't always assume that you need the depreciation deduction—always review the issues with a professional tax advisor before proceeding.

Pitfalls

A joint ownership arrangement can be problematic if the resident does not maintain the property or make the mortgage, insurance, or property tax payments. Furthermore, if the property does not go up in value, the nonresident party who put up the credit or cash may not realize any profits. Like any real estate investment, the shared equity arrangement should be approached with profit and not just financing in mind. In other words, make sure you buy the property at a good price and/or in the right neighborhood at the right time.

Alternatives to Equity Sharing

For the nonresident investor, there are several alternatives to the equity-sharing arrangement. The first is the lease option, which is discussed in more detail in the Chapter 8. The second is a joint venture.

Joint Ventures

A *joint venture* is a limited-purpose general partnership. A general partnership is formed when two or more people engage in a business with the intention of sharing profits and losses. A partnership need not necessarily be in writing, although it is generally a good idea. A joint venture is a general partnership that is limited in scope. Thus, if two individuals agree to buy a particular property with the intention of making a profit, the two individuals are not necessarily in business to buy properties; the scope of the partnership is limited to that one venture.

Under the federal tax code, a joint venture participation in a rental property does not necessarily create a partnership. So, while two individuals may co-own a rental property, they do not necessarily have to file a partnership return. However, if two or more individuals engage in multiple rental property investments, this may trigger reporting for federal tax purposes. For more information on partnership tax reporting, read IRS Publication 541 (get a free download at <www.irs.gov>).

Using Joint Venture Partnerships for Financing

Joint venture partnerships can be an excellent way to finance a real estate transaction, and they can be handled in a variety of ways. The most common is where one partner puts up cash and the other puts up his or her interest in the deal and/or his services in managing the property. The joint venture agreement will spell out how the money is contributed and how it is disbursed. Title to the property is generally held in the name of the joint venture, although title can be taken in the name of one or both of the partners. Using a partner to finance deals can be very effective on a deal-by-deal transaction.

Sometimes a joint venture partnership looks more like a general partnership because it is not specific to any one particular property. For example, an investor, or group of investors, may "pool" money together for the purchase of properties at a foreclosure auction. This type of arrangement should be approached with extreme caution because it looks more like a general partnership than a joint venture. It also may cross over into securities regulations, particularly if you are the one soliciting money from other investors.

Legal Issues

Owning real estate jointly with other parties is an effective financing tool, but it can also be a liability. Under the Uniform Partnership Act, the law holds all partners liable for each other's actions. Thus, if you are a "silent" partner, you could be held liable as the "deep pocket." Consider setting up a limited liability company (LLC) or limited partnership for joint venture projects. The owners of an LLC are shielded from liability for activities of the company and the activities of each other. Limited partners (but not general partners) of a limited partnership are similarly shielded from personal liability.

For more information on LLCs and limited partnerships, visit my Web site at <www.legalwiz.com/LLC>.

Alternative Arrangement for Partnership

Rather than having a partnership own the property, partners can realize the same profit goals by using a note and security instrument. One partner will hold title to the property and sign a note to the other partner for the amount of the other partner's cash investment. The note is secured by a mortgage on the property. A second note and mortgage is also executed, which will be a shared equity mortgage. A *shared equity mortgage* has a payoff that is based on a formula that relates to the increase in value of the property.

Shared equity mortgages (a.k.a. shared appreciation mortgages or participation mortgages) were popular when interest rates were so high that commercial borrowers could not maintain positive cash flow.

The lender thus dropped the interest rate in return for a share of the future profits in the borrower's property. Today, shared equity mortgages are not as popular, but they are still an effective tool for financing properties with people who are open-minded.

Tax Issue for the Lender

Normally, an investor must pay profits when he or she sells investment property for a gain. An owner (or co-owner) of real estate can defer paying taxes on this gain by exchanging under Section 1031 of the Internal Revenue Code. Because the partner holding the shared appreciation mortgage is not an owner of the real estate, he or she is not able to take advantage of a Section 1031 exchange (for more information on tax-deferred exchanging, go to <www.1031x.com>).

Case Study: Shared Equity Mortgage with Seller

A viable option for seller financing is to make the seller your partner with a shared appreciation mortgage. In this case, the seller/lender shares in the future appreciation of the property. A seller may be willing to accept little or nothing down in exchange for principal and interest payments, lack of management, and future appreciation. Essentially, the note and mortgage documents read the same as a standard note and mortgage, except that the payoff amount increases over time in proportion to the value of the property. The shared appreciation can be written a number of ways and need not necessarily be a 50/50 split of future appreciation.

Is a Shared Equity Mortgage a Partnership?

When using shared equity mortgages, there is a fine line between a lender/borrower and a partner/partner relationship. There could be adverse tax and legal consequences if a court or the IRS were to recharacterize a lender/borrower relationship to that of a legal partnership. The key legal distinction is the sharing of losses by the lender in the transaction. Because a partnership involves the agreed sharing of profits and losses, removing the lender's risk of loss will help avoid the recharacterization. As with any complicated transaction, you should hire the services of a competent attorney to draft or review the paperwork.

When Does a Partnership Not Make Sense?

Real estate partnerships, like any business partnership, should be approached with profit in mind. Buying property jointly with a friend makes no sense just because you want to limit your exposure to half the loss. Likewise, buying property with a partner should be avoided if the partner's share of the profit is less than you could pay for a loan. Even at 18 percent interest and with 10 points origination fee, you might still end up with more profit by borrowing hard money. Use your common sense and a calculator, not your emotions and fears.

An equity partner should be used when conventional, hard-money, seller-carryback, and creative financing means are out of the question. In my experience, if you need a partner to finance the deal, it may not be all that good a deal; if you buy at the right price, borrowing the necessary money is easy. However, there is one exception to this rule: If your partner has a great deal more experience than you, giving up part of the profit for a good education may be worthwhile. And, suffice it to say, make sure you know who you are partnering with by checking out his or her background and references.

Key Points

- Equity sharing and joint ventures can be effective financing alternatives.

- Approach general partnerships with extreme caution.

- Consider alternatives to partnerships whenever possible.

The Lease Option

The road less traveled is that way for a reason.

—Fortune Cookie

The lease-option strategy is a great way to leverage your real estate investments because it requires very little cash. The lease-option method is more of a financing alternative than a financing strategy because you don't own the property.

The basic lease-option strategy involves two legal documents, a lease agreement and an option. A lease gives you the right to possess the property, or, as an investor, to have someone else occupy it. If you can obtain a lease on a property at below market rent, you can profit by subleasing it at market rent.

An *option* is the right to buy a property. It is a unilateral or one-way agreement wherein the seller obligates himself or herself to sell you the property, but you are not obligated to buy it. By obtaining the right to buy, you control the property. You can market the property and sell it for a profit. The longer you can control the property in an appreciating market, the more value you create for yourself. By combining a lease and an option, you create a lease option.

Financing Alternative

The two primary objectives of the real estate investor are cash flow and appreciation. You don't need to own a property to create cash flow or benefit from appreciation. Because a lease entitles you to possession, it allows you to create cash flow. An option gives you the right to buy at a set price, allowing you to benefit from future appreciation.

Lease—The Right to Possession

Under a lease agreement, the lessor (landlord) gives the lessee (tenant) the right to possess and enjoy the property, one of the most important benefits of real estate ownership. The lessee is usually not responsible for property taxes and major repairs. Once you have the right to obtain possession of property, you can profit by subletting or assigning your right to possession.

Sublease

A *sublease* is a lease by a tenant to another person, a subtenant, of a part of the premises held by the tenant under a lease. The sublease can be for part of the premises or part of the time period. For example, if the tenant has a three-year lease agreement with the landlord, the tenant can sublease the rental unit for two years, or sublease part of the unit for three years.

Assignment

An *assignment* is a transfer to another of the whole of any property or any estate or right therein. As with a sublease, the master tenant is not relieved from liability for obligations under the lease. However, the assignee of a lease is in contract with the landlord, and thus the landlord can collect from the assignee *or* the master tenant for nonpayment of rent.

Assignment and subletting are always permissible without an express provision in the lease forbidding the tenant from doing so. As a tenant/investor, it is imperative that there are no antiassignment or antisubletting clauses in your lease with the owner of the property.

More on Options, the "Right" to Buy

A real estate sales contract is a *bilateral,* or two-way, agreement. The seller agrees to sell, and the purchaser agrees to buy. Compare this agreement with an option; an option is a *unilateral* contract in which the seller is obligated to sell, but the purchaser is not obligated to buy. On the other hand, if the purchaser on a bilateral contract refuses to buy, he or she can be held liable for damages.

A bilateral contract with contingency is similar to an option. Many contracts contain contingencies, which, if not met, result in the termination of the contract. Essentially, a bilateral contract with a contingency in favor of the purchaser turns a bilateral contract into an option in that it gives the purchaser an "out" if he or she decides not to purchase the property. Though the two are not legally the same, an option and a bilateral purchase contract with a contingency yield the same practical result.

The receiver of the option (*optionee*) typically pays the giver of the option (*optionor*) some nonrefundable option consideration, that is, money or other value for the right to buy. If the option is exercised, the relationship between the optionor and optionee becomes a binding, bilateral agreement between seller and buyer. In most cases, the option consideration is credited towards the purchase price of the property. If the option is not exercised, the optionee forfeits the option money.

As seen in the following examples, an option can be used to gain control of a property without actually owning it:

- A speculator who is aware of a proposed development can obtain options on farmland and then sell the options to developers.

- To take advantage of appreciation in a hot real estate market, an investor can use a long-term option to purchase property.

- To induce timely rental payments, a landlord can offer the tenant an option to purchase.

There are literally hundreds of ways that an option can be structured, and every detail is open for negotiation between the optionor (seller) and optionee (buyer).

An Option Can Be Sold or Exercised

An option, like a real estate purchase agreement, is a personal right that is assignable. If you were able to obtain an option to purchase at favorable terms, you could sell your option. The assignee of the option would then stand in your shoes, having the same right to exercise the option to purchase the property. As with a lease, an option is freely assignable absent an express provision in the option agreement to the contrary.

Alternative to Selling Your Option

Rather than sell your option to purchase, you may wish to exercise the option yourself, then sell the property to a third-party buyer in a double closing, as described in Chapter 5.

> **Famous Option Story**
>
> The most infamous option financing story is how the United Nations found its way to New York City. In the mid-1940s, William Zeckendorf, a now infamous developer, took options on multiple waterfront lots on the east side of Manhattan. At the time, the properties were primarily being used for slaughterhouses. Zeckendorf's option price for the lots was $6.5 million. With the help of the Rockefeller family, the United Nations purchased the property from Zeckendorf for $8.5 million.

The Lease Option

A lease option is really two transactions: a lease and an option to purchase. Under a lease, a tenant may have the option to buy the property. The option itself can be structured in various ways. For example, the option may be that of a right of first refusal in the event the landlord intends to sell the property. The option may also be an exclusive option for the tenant to buy at a certain price. When combined with a lease, a purchase option may also include rent credits, that is, an agreement that part of the monthly rent payments will be applied to reduce the purchase price of the property. There are literally hundreds of ways that an option or lease option can be structured, and every detail is open for negotiation between the landlord and tenant.

The Lease Purchase

The lease purchase, like a lease option, is two transactions: a lease and a purchase agreement. A regular purchase contract is a binding bilateral agreement; the seller agrees to sell and the buyer agrees to buy. An option binds the seller to sell, but the buyer is not bound to buy. If the buyer on a bilateral contract fails to buy, he or she is in breach of contract. However, a properly drafted agreement will limit the seller's legal remedy to simply keeping the buyer's earnest money (called a "liquidated damages clause"). Thus, as a practical matter, the result is the same as if the buyer gave nonrefundable option money and failed to exercise his or her option.

In practice, lease purchase and lease option are just buzzwords that mean the same thing. Except as noted, we will use the two terms throughout this book interchangeably.

Lease Option of Your Personal Residence

Pride of ownership is what makes so many Americans obsessed with the idea of owning a home. Once you get over this idea, you will see that you can often rent more home than you can buy.

Why buy when you can rent? We've all seen the ads used by real estate agents: "Why rent when you can buy?" Consider the other side of the coin: "Why buy when you can rent?" In most parts of the country, a typical $100,000 house will rent for about $1,000 per month. Assuming a reasonable down payment and interest rate, the monthly mortgage payments would be less than $1,000 per month. In this case, it makes sense to own the home. However, more expensive homes don't rent as well as cheaper homes. A typical $500,000 home does not rent for $5,000 per month. The more expensive the home, the cheaper it becomes to rent compared to buy. If you are concerned about the proverbial "throwing away rent," consider a lease option of your next home.

Case Study: Lease Option Builds Equity. A student of mine from the Phoenix area (we'll call her Sharon) was interested in purchasing a home to live in, but she didn't have much cash. She was at her new job just a short time and could not qualify for a conventional or an FHA low-down-payment loan. Sharon found a seller with a nice property, with little equity but with a low-interest-rate loan. Sharon leased the property from the owner for three years for $1,200 per month, with an option to buy at $162,000. The agreement provided that the seller give her a 25 percent ($300) credit towards the purchase price for each rent payment made. Sharon put up just $500 as a security deposit that would be credited toward the purchase price when she exercised her option to purchase.

After 18 months, the property had appreciated $17,000 in value to $179,000. In addition, Sharon's "equity" had increased $5,400 because of the $300 per month rent credit. Thus, Sharon's equity position was almost $23,000:

$162,000 Option price
\- 5,400 Rent credit
\-   500 Security deposit
$156,100 "Strike price"

$179,000 Market value
\-156,100 Strike price
$ 22,900 "Equity"

Sharon exercised her option to purchase the property and sold it to a third party, pocketing the cash difference.

A few points are worth noting here: First, had Sharon purchased the home 18 months earlier, she would have been required by the lender to put up several thousand dollars for a down payment and loan costs. Because Sharon intended to live in the property for just a few years, she maximized her profit by using a lease option to control the property for 18 months, rather than a mortgage loan.

Second, Sharon's risk is limited to her $500 investment. If Sharon had bought the property with conventional financing and property values had declined over the 18-month period, Sharon would have been stuck with the property. As you can see, using options to leverage real estate is an effective alternative to bank financing when future real estate values are uncertain.

Lease Option REFI

Rather than sell the property, Sharon in our Case Study could have obtained a loan to buy the property. In doing so, most lenders would consider the transaction a purchase and lend basing their LTV on the option strike price ($156,100), not the appraised value ($179,000). A small number of lenders will treat the transaction as a refinance (REFI), in which case the LTV is based on the appraised value. So, a 90 percent LTV refinance would allow a lender to give Sharon .9 × $179,000 = $161,000, which would cover the strike price and the loan costs. Because a lease option REFI is not an ordinary transaction, be patient if you are looking for a lender that will fund in this manner; it will take a lot of phone calls!

Also note that some lenders will only permit a rent credit to the extent that the rent paid exceeds the normal market rent for that house. Thus, you may not get away with having 50% of the rent credited towards purchase to satisfy a lender's down payment requirement.

The Sandwich Lease Option

The sandwich lease option is an old technique used by real estate entrepreneurs to create cash, cash flow, and equity buildup with literally no money, credit, or bank loans.

Let me give you a typical example of how a sandwich lease option works. A seller (soon to be *landlord*) is transferred out of town and rents his property. A year later, the tenant vacates (after skipping a few months rent) and leaves a big mess. The owner wants to sell the property for $110,000. It is the middle of the winter, the house is vacant, and the real estate market is a bit slow.

The house needs new paint and carpet and therefore looks ugly. The $850 per month mortgage payment is a burden to the owner. He decides to lease it on a month-to-month basis but cannot find a tenant because nobody wants to lease a house for sale when he or she may have to leave within a few months. The owner is a perfect candidate for a lease option.

The potential buyer (a.k.a. tenant) filed for bankruptcy two years ago. He just moved to town. Although he has stable income, he cannot yet qualify for a loan. In addition, he still has to sell his old house to raise some cash for the down payment. He doesn't really want a straight rental, yet he is not ready to buy today. The tenant is a perfect candidate for the other end of a lease option. See Figure 8.1.

Cash Flow

So how do we, as real estate investors, fit in? Find the owner who fits the picture and sign up a lease-option agreement wherein you are the tenant/buyer. You are not going to live in the property but are still considered a "master tenant." The lease-option agreement will give you the right to sublet the property. If the price you pay is lower than market rent, you can create cash flow by subletting the property to another tenant. Depending on the deal, this can create several hundred dollars per month of cash flow—not bad for a property you don't even own!

Equity Buildup

After a year or two, you may have accumulated some equity in one of the following ways:

- Appreciation of the property due to inflation

- Increase in value from improvements on the property

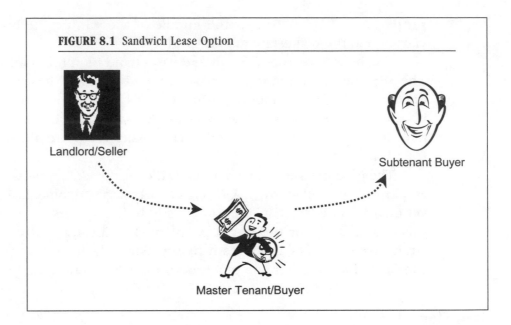

FIGURE 8.1 Sandwich Lease Option

Landlord/Seller

Subtenant Buyer

Master Tenant/Buyer

- Increase in equity from rent credits offered by the landlord/ seller

Once your *equity,* the difference between the market value and your option strike price, reaches around 10 percent, you can obtain lender financing and buy the property. Or, you can offer the property for sale to another investor. Better yet, offer the property for sale to the tenant. In many cases, a tenant/buyer is willing to pay more than the property is worth! When the tenant is ready to exercise his option, you exercise your option from the owner and sell it to the tenant in a back-to-back double closing for a profit.

Straight Option without the Lease

A purchase option can be used without a lease to gain control of a property and create a profit. Once you have obtained an option, you can either sell (assign) your option for immediate profit or exercise your option to purchase and simultaneously sell it to a third-party buyer. If you are speculating that a particular area is ripe for development, you can use an option as a long-term investment technique.

An option is a leveraged, low-risk investment; you can obtain an option with 1 percent or less of the purchase price in cash. Again, using options in lieu of conventional financing is cheaper and less risky when you are dealing with a real estate market that has an uncertain future.

Case Study: Sandwich Lease Option

I was referred to a woman who had a house she needed to sell in a hurry because she had a job transfer. She had tried to sell the property with a real estate agent, but, at the last minute, the buyer could not qualify for a new loan.

The house was a small two-bedroom ranch that was worth approximately $45,000. The balance of the existing loan was approximately $38,000, with monthly payments of $380 per month (including taxes and insurance escrows). Although the average rents in the neighborhood were about $575, she was not interested in becoming a long-distance landlord.

I offered to lease the property for $380 per month, with an option to purchase at $38,000 (the balance owed on her mortgage loan). I had the right to sublet, but I explained to her that my payments to her were not contingent on occupancy. This alleviated her fear of having to deal with the property if it became vacant.

I subletted the property for market rent, which was $575. After about two years, the market value of the property had risen to $75,000, so I exercised my option to buy at $38,000. Based on a $75,000 appraisal, I had no problem obtaining solid, institutional financing for the property. In fact, I even pulled out $4,000 from the refinance to make capital improvements to the property. My payments went up, but so did the rents, based on the improvements and increase in value of the neighborhood.

Obviously, the payments on a $400,000 house will be different, but the concept is the same. For more information on using lease options, take a look at my home study package, "Big Profits with Lease options," at <www.legalwiz.com>.

Sale-Leaseback

The sale-leaseback is a financing technique that has been used in the United States since the 1940s. The transaction, in its most basic form, involves the sale of a property to an investor who holds title and leases the property back to the former owner. The lease is typically a long-term net lease with the seller/tenant having the option of repurchasing at a later time. The seller/tenant reaps the benefit of favorable 100 percent "financing" and still retains the use of the property.

The buyer/landlord receives the tax benefit of depreciation and a guaranteed long-term rental. To do this with nothing down, simply sign a contract to purchase the property from the seller, then another contract to sell it to an investor. In a double closing, you purchase the property from the seller and resell it to the investor, who then leases it back to you, giving you an option to repurchase. You can then rent it out for cash flow or sublease it with an option to a tenant/buyer as described previously in this chapter.

The sale-leaseback has its drawbacks. If either party to a sale-leaseback is audited, the IRS may recharacterize the sale-leaseback as a disguised financing arrangement. This will result in an immediate recapture of the buyer/landlord's depreciation of the property and imputed interest on the seller/tenant's rental payments. The seller/tenant will lose the deduction for his or her rental payments because the payments will be reclassified as principal repayment of a loan.

The United States Supreme Court, in the landmark case of *Frank Lyon Co.* v. *United States,* stated the factors to be considered for recharacterization are

- the economic substance of the transaction based upon the potential risks and gains of the parties, and

- whether there was a purpose other than tax avoidance for the transaction.

While the above standards set forth by the court are not crystal clear, following are a few guidelines that we can follow to avoid recharacterization:

- Make certain that the purchase price of the property is for fair market value.

- Make certain the lease payments are for fair market rent, and that the lease arrangement is typical of the area and the intended use.

- Have reasons (other than tax avoidance) for the transaction and state those reasons in the preamble of your agreement.

- If the seller/tenant has an option to repurchase, make certain that it is based upon fair market value and not on a declining basis with unusually large rent credits (i.e., make sure it doesn't look like a loan payoff).

- Make certain that the buyer/landlord has the rights of any typical landlord in a comparable lease arrangement (including the right to have the property back at the end of the lease!).

Make certain that there is nothing in the sale-leaseback arrangement that prevents the buyer/landlord from selling, mortgaging, or assigning his or her interest or benefiting from future appreciation of the property.

Case Study: Sale-Leaseback

A client of mine (we'll call him Chris) used a sale-leaseback to profit in a win/win arrangement with a builder. The builder had finished developing the first phase of a new housing project. The builder's lender wanted to make sure a majority of the houses from the first phase were complete before extending the builder more credit to build the second phase.

Chris offered to purchase the model homes the builder used to show to prospective purchasers. Chris and the builder entered into a sale-leaseback agreement, wherein Chris bought the properties at 80 percent of fair market value, then leased the properties back to the builder to use as model homes. Because the builder was able to show his lender that three of the homes in the first phase of the subdivision were sold, the builder was allowed to borrow more money for the next phase of the development. By the time the third phase of the development was complete, the builder no longer needed the model homes. The property values had increased, and Chris sold the homes for a substantial profit.

Key Points

- The lease option is an excellent, high-leverage financing alternative.

- The sandwich lease option is a cash flow generator.

- The sale-leaseback is another excellent financing alternative.

CHAPTER 9

Investor Financing Pitfalls

"Experience is the name everyone gives to their mistakes."

–Oscar Wilde

Throughout this book we have discussed "OPM," the concept of using other people's money to finance investment properties. There's an additional concept to add, which is using "OPE"—other people's experience. Experience often comes from mistakes, which many others have made, us included. Mistakes are learning experiences that allow you to grow if you are willing to learn from them. Don't be afraid to make mistakes if you are willing to chalk them up as "experience."

However, don't be stubborn either; you can learn just as much from other people's mistakes (experiences) as well. This chapter is extremely important because it comes from the years of experience in financing properties, both as a principal and for our clients. Read this chapter twice, as it will save you from making common mistakes that can result in getting your loan application denied.

Listing before You Refinance

A big mistake that investors often make is listing a property for sale and then trying to refinance the property after it won't sell. If you decide you would like to take equity from the property, do not list the property for sale. Lenders are leery about giving borrowers money for property that was listed on the MLS and didn't sell.

Appraisers have access to the MLS and check to see if a property was previously listed. Because the vast majority of properties sell through the MLS system, it is a very good indicator of true market value. Thus, if a property was listed for 90 days in a market where the average time on the market is 60 days, there is good reason to question the value of the property. It's one thing to say a property is theoretically worth $200,000, but if it doesn't sell on the open market for that price within a reasonable time period, then it's probably not worth $200,000. If you try to refinance based on a $200,000 value, chances are the appraisal will come back much lower.

You should decide your "exit" strategy before you purchase the property. If you use bridge financing, then intend to keep it as a rental, you are going to need to refinance the debt you used to acquire the property. If you buy a fixer, for example, then improve the value, you can get a loan based on an appraisal of the new (increased) value of the property.

☛ **Example:** You purchase a property for $150,000 that needs $15,000 in rehab. When complete, the property should sell for $200,000, but in its "as is" condition, it will only appraise for $175,000. After the rehab, you are into the property for $165,000, you refinance for 80 percent of the new value ($200,000), and you end up with a $160,000 loan, thus only $5,000 actually comes out of your pocket.

However, if you listed the property on the MLS for $200,000 for several months and it did not sell, you are likely to get an appraisal for $190,000 or less, meaning you can only borrow $152,000 (80% of $190,000), in which case your out-of-pocket expense is $13,000.

The lesson here is to be careful about showing value if you intend to refinance the property. Appraisals are opinions of value, but the people who review the appraisals look at the real market to determine whether they want to lend. In some cases you can justify the value despite your listing price that didn't result in a sale, but it is difficult to convince a loan underwriter if you bought the property for 25 percent less just a few months ago.

Borrowing When You Need It

There is a saying in the loan business: "Banks only lend to people who don't need the money." There is some truth to this. If you have gainful employment, proof of income, a good credit score, and plenty of assets, most any bank is willing to lend you money. The moment you decide to become a full-time investor, you are no longer employed. There are ways to prove income as a self-employed person, but you must show that you are in business for two years.

Therefore, how do you prove that you have been in business for two years? The easiest way to show you are in business for two years is to show the income tax returns from your business for two years. This is a Catch-22 situation, however. If you are working a regular salaried position, you won't have a Schedule C on your federal income tax return to show you are in business. The second way is to get a letter from your accountant stating that you have been in business two years, which many lenders accept in lieu of tax returns (particularly if the loan you are applying for does not require verification of income). However, most accountants will not write such a letter if it is not true, because this could result in liability for conspiring to commit loan fraud.

The third way is to actually be in business two years. Most lenders will accept a business license or corporate documentation showing your company was formed at least two years ago. It is recommended that you form an LLC (limited liability company) or corporation right away, so that when you decide to go full-time you can show proof of being in business two years. Many incorporation outfits actually sell "aged" corporations that have been in business two years or more for this purpose. Be careful how you represent this to your lender because having a business that is two years old and *being* in business two years are two very different things.

Finally, if you are employed full-time and moving towards going full-time as an investor, make sure you apply for a HELOC while you can still prove income. Get the biggest HELOC you can, regardless of what the interest rate is because you want easy access to money for cash purchases.

Trying to Take Cash Out at Closing

Beyond buying "nothing down," there are actually legal ways to take money out of a closing when you purchase or refinance a property. First, understand that it is illegal to directly take cash at closing without it being disclosed on the HUD Settlement Statement. Many investors get cash back at closing through a variety of illegal means, with the approval, and often at the suggestion of their mortgage or real estate broker. These methods include:

- Inflating the purchase price and writing checks outside of closing

- Paying off bogus contractors that are actually the buyer's company

- Taking part of the real estate agent's commission after closing (without disclosing it on the HUD-1)

- Having the seller promise the buyer certain repairs or improvements after closing and then writing checks instead of doing the repairs

There are many varieties, but they all have something in common:

1. It is prearranged by the parties.

2. It is not disclosed on the HUD.

3. It is done over and over between the same parties.

In reality, all you need to do is caught get once and you may be prosecuted for loan fraud. In most cases, however, the investors who are the dumbest are the ones who do it over and over, figuring if they got away with it once, they can get away with it twice, three times, and so on. The point is that it is not illegal *per se* to take cash from a party after the closing for one reason or another, such as demanding cash from a seller after he did not perform certain repairs as promised. However, if you "coincidentally" do it over and over, it establishes in the contract a pattern of fraud that any prosecutor can follow and make a case against you. If you do take cash out of closing in a way that looks like fraud, make sure you have legitimate documentation to back it up. Lawyers use the "straight-faced argument" test, that is, if you get caught and hailed into court, can you go before a judge and explain what you are doing with a straight face? If you can't establish a legitimate reason for what you are doing, then don't do it.

There are some legal ways to take cash out of closing, within reason. For example, you can refinance a property for more than you owe, so long as the lender knows it is a "cash out" transaction. Too many investors try to pull all of the equity out of the property, which is difficult, not to mention risky if market values are flattening or falling.

Because most lenders would prefer a noncash out transaction, you can also establish a legitimate lien on the property using a mortgage or deed of trust securing a note or line of credit in favor of an entity that you own. This way, the lien that gets paid off at closing is to your entity, not to you, and thus is not considered "cash out." Make certain your affiliation with this entity is not hidden from the lender, and is supported by "arms'-length" loan documentation. Whatever you do, make sure you are not misrepresenting or concealing any material fact on your loan application or closing documents, otherwise the lender may report you to the Feds for loan fraud.

There's a fine line between tax avoidance and tax evasion; likewise, the line often becomes blurred between "creative" financing and loan fraud. You are ultimately responsible for your signature on a document, so do not let yourself be bullied by a mortgage broker, real estate broker, or anyone else who says, "Everybody does it this way."

Not Inspecting the Property Properly

One of the biggest deal killers is a last-minute inspection of the property by the lender's appraiser that results in a big surprise, such as:

- Faulty wiring or plumbing

- Termites

- Asbestos

- The home was used as a meth lab

- A manufactured home

- Structural defects

In some cases, a property becomes uninsurable because of a bad roof or because the property has extensive water damage. There is a national risk database that insurers look to for past insurance claims called "CLUE" (Comprehensive Loss Underwriting Exchange). Only the seller can order the report, so if you are buying you can require a CLUE report as part of your purchase offer from *www.choicetrust.com.*

Many investors buy properties "sight unseen" from another investor, through a foreclosure, tax sale, estate, or other situation where the property has been vacant and may have some serious problems. Novice investors often buy properties using private money or their own cash, so there's no "required" inspection, often leading to disastrous results when they try to refinance or resell the property to someone else who applies for a loan secured by a mortgage on the property.

Unless you are a qualified general contractor you should hire a licensed professional to inspect the property. You may be trying to save some money, however a few hundred dollars spent now will save you thousands later. You can get a referral from a local real estate broker or from the American Society of Home Inspectors (*see www.ashi.org*).

Not Knowing Your Comps

Knowing value is probably one of the biggest issues when purchasing and financing real estate. Investors often underestimate repairs and overestimate the value the property will have after it is repaired. The appraisal may not come in as high as you like for the financing of the resale or refinancing, and you have to be prepared to face this issue.

Keep in mind than an appraiser is only giving an opinion of value, he or she is not the person purchasing the property. As we discussed in Chapter 3, an appraiser looks at comparable sales of properties to determine the value of the property. In the case of a purchase, the appraiser looks at the contract price as an indication of value to justify the appraisal, unless the purchase price is completely out of line for the neighborhood. Thus, it is your job to know all of the relevant sales history in the neighborhood to show the appraiser, as well as the loan officers that may be reviewing the appraisal. If you cannot find comparable sales in your neighborhood, you can show comparable sales in neighborhoods in nearby areas. An appraiser will generally consider comparable sales up to a mile away, unless you are in a densely populated urban area that drastically differs from block to block. In vastly rural areas, an appraiser will allow for more than a mile, but this is unusual.

Lenders are often skeptical when a property was purchased recently for a substantially lower price, even if it was a rehab property. You should gather as much documentation as you can to show the appraiser and the loan underwriters that you did substantial work to improve the value of the property. If you purchased the property in a distress situation such as a foreclosure, estate, or divorce, make sure you have documentation to demonstrate why you purchased the property at a reduced purchase price.

Saying the Wrong Things on Your Loan Application

Saying the wrong things on your loan application may kill your chances of getting a loan. Like filling out a tax return, there are several ways to present your financial picture on a loan application. Some things are black and white, such as how much you earned in W-2 income last year. Other things are a matter of interpretation, such as the number of years you have been working in a particular line of business.

Your job is to make your loan application look as favorable as possible to the lender, without lying, misleading, or hiding anything materially negative. Other than your credit and the collateral for the loan, lenders want to see income, job stability, and liquid-cash reserves.

Most investor loans are based on "stated" income. In this case, an investor lists his or her income on the loan application without having to show W-2s or tax returns as proof. This may be beneficial for people in their own businesses and/or if their income comes from many sources. Besides the potential criminal implications of lying on your application, the chances of it actually being approved may decrease if it is not believable. Loan underwriters often use *www.salary.com* or equivalent to determine if the borrower's income is reasonable considering the line of work he or she is in. This is another place where being "creative" helps on your application. Let's say you are an insurance claims adjuster and you own and operate several rental properties. Which profession are you in? If you spend a substantial amount of your time dealing with your real estate, maybe you are better off saying you are a property manager. According to *www.salary.com*, the average income for a property manager is much higher than an insurance claims adjuster's is.

There is no correct answer, but what you must be aware of is that lenders don't accept what you report as gospel. Moreover, keep in mind that if you apply for another loan with the same lender a few months later, they may notice if the income you are reporting has changed substantially. Also, the lender may look at the number of properties you have acquired since your last loan. If you have only been investing in real estate a few years and start buying too many properties too quickly, it may be a cause for alarm that you are getting in over your head.

The bottom line is you should ask for help from a qualified mortgage broker or banker in filling out your loan application. On the one hand, you don't want to let someone talk you into stating things that aren't true, but having someone with experience at presenting favorable loan packages can be helpful.

Not Reading the Fine Print

Too many investors go to closing and sign documents without ever reading them, taking the word of the "professionals" involved in the closing. This is a huge mistake, unless that professional is your lawyer, and he or she has read and understood the loan documents. Don't presume that the lawyer you are paying represents you. Many banks have lawyers that represent them and charge that fee to the borrower.

Mortgage brokers and lenders are not by their nature dishonest but there are enough shady characters that try to slip things by on borrowers. In some cases, it is a mistake by the lender or a miscommunication between the mortgage broker and the lender, both of which result in the borrower getting a different loan than what was promised.

The most common things that are incorrect on a loan are:

- **Prepayment Penalty.** The most common "hidden" clause is a prepayment penalty that the lender does not disclose or that was supposed to be omitted. The only way to know for sure is to read your mortgage note to see if there is a prepayment penalty clause. In some cases, a lender may say there is no prepayment penalty, but has inserted a "soft" prepayment penalty (see Chapter 4 for a discussion of soft versus hard prepayment penalties). In addition, read carefully how much the penalty is, and how long after the loan is originated the penalty applies.

- **Fixed versus Adjustable Rate.** If you pay for a fixed-rate loan, you may end up with a surprise at closing in the form of an adjustable-rate loan that is fixed only for a certain time period, such as two years. In some cases, you may be promised a five-year fixed rate and end up with a three-year fixed rate. Moreover, read carefully about how the loan adjusts. Some ARM loans can only be adjusted twice a year, others can be adjusted monthly. Finally, look at the amount the loan can adjust each time, and the maximum rate the lender can charge over the life of the loan. All of this will be spelled out in the mortgage note. (Hint: if the note is titled, "Adjustable Rate Loan," it's a dead giveaway that you don't have a fixed-rate loan!)

- **Owner-Occupied Loan.** If you apply for the loan as investor, the mortgage broker may submit it for approval as an owner-occupied loan, either by accident or on purpose. Read the documents carefully. Do not sign your name to any document saying that you promise to live in the property if you aren't actually going to do so. In most cases, the mortgage or deed of trust will have a rider (addendum) that says you do not intend to occupy the property as your principal residence. Most investors think that lenders won't find out, but they often do check, so you risk getting caught and prosecuted for loan fraud.

Not Knowing Your Exit Strategy before You Buy

As we discussed in our book *Defensive Real Estate Investing* (Kaplan 2007), you need to know your exit strategy before you buy. In fact, it helps to have more than one exit strategy. For example, if you intend to resell the property to an owner-occupant, you need to make sure the property will qualify for a loan. As we discussed in Chapter 5, HUD regulations require that the seller own the property for at least 90 days for the property to qualify for an FHA loan. Many subprime lenders require six months or more of title "seasoning." If you change your mind and refinance the property to keep it as a rental, will the loan you used to acquire the property suffice, or will you need to refinance the property to get a low enough payment to rent it? If you sell it on the back end on a lease/option, will the property appraise for the option price you have offered to your tenant now, or in two years when the option period is up?

The lesson here is that you must consider your back end before you purchase the property so that you know what your financing options are, as well as the financing options of your buyer.

Applying for Credit during a Loan

Keep in mind that a lender pulls your credit twice during the loan process; once at the beginning and then again just before closing. If any new debt or negative items show up in the meantime, this appears on your report and may delay or even prevent you from closing on your loan. Your lender even looks at new inquiries on your credit file to see if you applied for another credit line, mortgage loan, or other debt that was not reported on your loan application. If your credit was pulled and there's no corresponding loan, your lender wants to know why. If you applied elsewhere and were denied, there may be a reason that they know of that your current lender does not! Many borrowers also make the mistake of "shopping" for loans, having their credit pulled at different lenders to work one against the other for rates. This often backfires, so be careful of how many times your credit is pulled in a short period of time.

Building without Permits

Although investors often do rehabs without permits; you are technically required to get building permits from your local municipality. Some permits require a licensed contractor, while others can be done without a license. Depending on the scope of the work, a lender may require an inspection and certificate of occupancy ("C.O.") or certificate of completion ("C.O.C") from a local building department before lending against the property. In most parts of the country you can get away with cosmetic work and minor plumbing without a permit or a C.O.C. It is important that you discuss the scope of the work with a lender in your area to see what is customary.

Keep in mind that existing repairs done by the seller or a previous owner can trip you up as well. Investors often get blindsided by a requirement that a local housing inspector certify an existing addition or finished basement, even though someone else did the work years ago. In some cases, a lender may only require that the appraiser state in his or her appraisal that the previous improvements were done in a "workman-like" manner.

Key Points

- Be careful about listing a property on the MLS if you intend to refinance it

- Apply for a HELOC while you still have a job and provable income

- Taking cash out of closing is difficult, especially if you want to do it legally

- Learn how to properly prepare a loan application

- Read before you sign any loan documents

CHAPTER 10

Real Stories of Investor Financing

"God made man because He loves stories."

–Elie Wiesel

This chapter is a compilation of true stories about investor financing that illustrate the principles in this book. Some of them are personal stories of the authors and some of our clients, and the names have been changed to protect their privacy. Use these stories as both an inspiration and a way to remember the principles in this book so you can apply them to your own real estate investments.

Keep in mind that you may not be able to do each and every transaction the same, because loan underwriting guidelines change from time to time. However, it will give you "food for thought," so to speak, to think outside the box when trying to finance your investments.

"Nothing Down" Refinance

Bill bought a foreclosed house from a bank for $108,000. The property needed paint, carpet, and other miscellaneous items totaling $5,000. Bill estimated the value of the property to be $145,000 when the work was complete.

Bill bought the property in his own name using all cash as follows:

- **Step 1:** He borrowed $115,000 from his home equity line of credit on his personal residence.

- **Step 2:** He lent $115,000 to his LLC, documenting the loan with a promissory note.

- **Step 3:** His LLC lent $115,000 back to himself, documenting the loan with a promissory note signed by Bill and securing the loan with a mortgage on the property.

- **Step 4:** He purchased the property using the loan from his LLC as the source of funds, $115,000 ($7,000 more than the $108,000 purchase price).

- **Step 5:** He used $5,000 from the proceeds from the loan to fix the property, and the other $2,000 for closing costs.

- **Step 6:** He applied for a refinance from an institutional lender for 80 percent of the appraised value. The property appraised for $150,000, and he borrowed $120,000, which included a payoff of the existing $115,000 loan and the closing costs for the new loan.

- **Step 7:** At the closing of the refinance, the LLC was paid off for its $115,000 loan. The LLC then paid back the loan to Bill, and he paid off his line of credit, plus a few hundred bucks for interest.

In the end, the monthly payments on the new loan, including taxes and insurance, were about the same as the rent being collected. Certainly, there would be negative cash flow from time to time for vacancies and repairs, but this would be offset by the tax write-off for depreciation. In addition, the property had 20 percent equity and Bill had no cash out of pocket. Because a loan was being paid off when he refinanced (the loan from his LLC), this was not considered a "cash out" loan.

Keep in mind that information about your LLC is public record, so your lender should see your association with the entity. Either the title company or the lender faxes the LLC a request for loan payoff, which is signed by an officer or manager of the LLC, namely you. Don't try to conceal your affiliation with the LLC, otherwise your lender could make a case that you are trying to commit loan fraud.

"Flash Cash"

Joe was trying to do a double closing, buying a property in foreclosure and selling it simultaneously to an owner-occupant for a $24,000 profit. Because the property was in foreclosure, time was running out, and he wanted use the funds from the backend closing to fund his purchase, as described in Chapter 5. The lender for the buyer on the second closing insisted that Joe own the property before they would fund the second closing. In other words, Joe was not able to do a simultaneous closing using the funds from the back end to fund the front end. Joe needed $180,000 cash for three minutes to close on the purchase before reselling the property for a $24,000 profit.

Joe borrowed $180,000 from another investor for "flash cash" to complete the transaction, paying 5 percent of the loan as a fee. Joe paid the investor $9,000 for using the investor's money for three minutes (actually, it took about three days for the title company to get the funds, close the deal, and refund the investor). The lesson here is that in a pinch, you sometimes have to be willing to give up some of your profit to get a deal done. In this case Joe still made $15,000 profit, which is pretty good money.

> If you are the investor putting up the "flash cash" be sure to do your due diligence:
>
> 1. Only lend money to investors who you know are experienced and have a good reputation. Although your money is only on the table for a few days, it can quickly turn into a few months if things go wrong.
> 2. Make sure you know the title company doing the closing so that they can assure you nothing is out of the ordinary. Make sure the title closer has specific written instructions not to release your funds to the seller until the backend deal is complete and ready to close back-to-back.

"Subject-to" Refinance

Bill found a seller with a property with a four-unit apartment building worth about $350,000 in foreclosure. The seller wanted to walk away with approximately $25,000, which included over six months of back payments to the lender. Bill gave the seller some cash, paid the loan current, and took title to the property subject to the $230,000 existing mortgage, for a total of about $255,000. After about a year, he refinanced the property based on appraisal value, paying off the existing loan, and recouping his out-of-pocket cash.

"Piggy-Back" Second

This is a variation on the "nothing down refinance" if you decide to keep the property as a rental and don't have the cash to purchase it outright up front. Oliver purchased a property for $152,000 that needed approximately $15,000 in repairs. The after-repaired value was estimated at $220,000. Oliver got two new loans for a total of $152,000 to purchase the property: an 80 percent first mortgage loan of $121,600 and a 10 percent second mortgage for $15,200. Oliver put up 10 percent cash ($15,200) as a down payment. Oliver then invested approximately $15,000 on repairs, using additional cash out of his pocket.

Oliver kept the first loan in place and then refinanced the second mortgage for a total of 90 percent of the after-repaired value ($121,600 first mortgage + $46,000 second mortgage).

In summary, Oliver put up $15,200 as a down payment, and $15,000 in repairs and another $5,000 in closing costs for the loans for a total out-of-pocket cash amount of $35,200. With the new second mortgage of $46,000, he walked away with a net of $10,800. More than likely, he will have some negative cash flow on the property; however he has cash in his pocket to make up for it, plus 10 percent equity. In an appreciating market, this is a good deal because the profit will be made when the property is resold in a few years. Be wary about doing a deal with negative cash flow if your local housing market is not on the upswing.

Partner Financing Using IRAs

Mary was buying properties subject to existing loans and reselling them via leases with options to purchase. A typical property was worth $200,000, and Mary would buy it subject to a $165,000 loan giving the seller $10,000. In some cases, the loan was in default, so the part of the $10,000 was paid directly to the lender for back payments. Mary would sell the property for $205,000 to $210,000 on a two-year lease/option.

Mary was running out of cash for these deals, so she went to investors and asked them to borrow the $10,000 for each deal directly from their self-directed IRA (discussed in Chapter 1). The investor would get a second mortgage lien on the property for their investment, paying

15 percent simple interest. When the property sold, Mary would make approximately $30,000 to $35,000 profit, less $1,500 per year in interest payments to the investors.

As with any deal in which you are lending money, make certain your money is evidenced by a note and properly secured by the property with a mortgage lien. Also, be careful about publicly soliciting investor money secured by guaranteed returns, as such an offering may require securities registration with the state or federal government.

Pre-Built Construction

Ronda purchased a condo from the builder for $550,000, using a 70 percent first mortgage and a 20 percent second mortgage. The builder agreed in the contract to pay two years of HOA fees and six months' worth of Ronda's mortgage payments in advance. The builder also paid for approximately several thousand dollars in upgrades and closing costs. While Ronda had to put some money up front for a down payment (10 percent), she would recoup this quickly from the increased cash flow over the next six months. These types of deals are possible because the builder has a great deal of profit and can make concessions to the borrower rather than drop the price of the unit.

Option ARM versus Fixed Rate

In 2001, Bob purchased a rental property worth approximately $350,000 in foreclosure for $250,000, subject to the existing loan, which was an adjustable rate mortgage that was currently at 8.75 percent. The monthly amortized payment for principal and interest was about $1,950, but the existing loan terms would allow the lender to raise the interest rate as high as 13 percent. The property had plenty of equity, so Bob had two choices for refinancing the loan: a fixed-rate mortgage at 8 percent or an option ARM loan starting at 1.75 percent.

The payment for a fixed loan at 8 percent interest amortized over 30 years would be $1,834.00 per month. After five years, the total payments for principal and interest would be about $110,000, of which about $15,000 would be principal reduction on the loan. The advantage here is certainty—there's no surprise about what the payment will or could be if interest rates go up.

As discussed in Chapter 4, an option ARM loan gives the borrower the option of paying four different ways each month. The payments are based on two factors, the loan index, such as the LIBOR (see Chapter 4 for a discussion of the different loan indexes) and the loan margin, which is the lender's profit above the index (usually 1.5 to 2.5 percent). The four choices for payments are:

- Minimum payment based on the initial rate, which is generally fixed for five or ten years

- 30-year amortization payment based on the loan index plus the loan margin

- 15-year amortization payment on the loan index plus the loan margin

- Interest-only payment on the loan index plus the loan margin

At the time, the initial rate was 1.75 percent, which was only $893/month. The interest-only and amortized payments were based on the index and the margin, which totaled about 4.5 percent—very attractive indeed. However, because the rate on this loan changes based on the index, there was the risk that the total rate on the loan could increase over time, resulting in a much higher payment for the interest-only or amortized payments. Bob could choose to continue making the minimum payment based on the initial rate, but in doing so would cause the loan balance to increase each month as the interest payments due were deferred. Bob purchased the property with a

30 percent equity position, so there was plenty of room for a negative-amortizing loan if Bob chose to make the minimum payment instead of the interest-only payment. This particular loan had a lifetime interest rate cap at 9.95 percent, and could only adjust a maximum of 2 percent per year, so there was no risk of a sudden jump in payments if the market rate of interest went up to 12%.

Bob chose to make the 30-year amortized payment each month, except for a few months when the property had high vacancy, at which time he paid the minimum payment. Without going into the complicated math, it's sufficient to say that over the last five years, Bob has paid far less for payments than he would have if the loan were fixed the entire time at 8 percent. Currently his interest rate (index + the margin) is about the same as market interest rates for a fixed-rate loan, so it is not worth refinancing.

The lesson here is that a fixed-rate loan is not necessarily better than an ARM loan for every borrower. It is important to read through all of the conditions and provisions of your ARM loan to see what the likely difference in payments is, and what the risks are if your assumptions are wrong. Over the last five years, many investors (and consumers) bought properties using ARM loans only considering the initial payment, not the worst-case scenario if interest rates went up based on the index, which they ultimately did. They also bought in markets where values did not increase, so as they made their minimum monthly payments, the principal balance exceeded the value of the property, leading to financial disaster. A smart investor should avoid financing properties based on the idea that interest rates will always be low and/or that values will always increase as they did in the past. Option ARM loans can be a good cash management tool, but should be used only if the property is purchased with a substantial equity position or the investor can survive another market cycle.

We hope that the case studies and other techniques you have learned in this book will save you money and create better opportunities to finance creative real state deals.

APPENDIX A

Interest Payments Chart

Interest Rate Chart
Monthly Payment per $1,000 Borrowed

Interest Rate %	15-Year Term	30-Year Term	Interest Rate %	15-Year Term	30-Year Term
4	7.40	4.77	8	9.56	7.34
4⅛	7.46	4.85	8⅛	9.63	7.42
4¼	7.52	4.92	8¼	9.70	7.51
4⅜	7.59	4.99	8⅜	9.77	7.60
4½	7.65	5.07	8½₈	9.85	7.69
4⅝	7.71	5.14	8⅝	9.92	7.78
4¾	7.78	5.22	8¾	9.99	7.87
4⅞	7.84	5.29	8⅞	10.07	7.96
5	7.91	5.37	9	10.14	8.05
5⅛	7.97	5.44	9⅛	10.22	8.14
5¼	8.04	5.52	9¼	10.29	8.23
5⅜	8.10	5.60	9⅜	10.37	8.32
5½	8.17	5.68	9½	10.44	8.41
5⅝	8.24	5.76	9⅝	10.52	8.50
5¾	8.30	5.84	9¾	10.59	8.59
5⅞	8.37	5.92	9⅞	10.67	8.68
6	8.44	6.00	10	10.75	8.77
6⅛	8.51	6.08	10⅛	10.82	8.87
6¼	8.57	6.16	10¼	10.90	8.96
6⅜	8.64	6.24	10⅜	10.98	9.05
6½	8.71	6.32	10½	11.05	9.15
6⅝	8.78	6.40	10⅝	11.13	9.24
6¾	8.85	6.48	10¾	11.21	9.33
6⅞	8.92	6.57	10⅞	11.29	9.43
7	8.99	6.65	11	11.36	9.52
7⅛	9.06	6.74	11⅛	11.44	9.62
7¼	9.13	6.82	11¼	11.52	9.71
7⅜	9.20	6.91	11⅜	11.60	9.81
7½	9.27	6.99	11½	11.68	9.90
7⅝	9.34	7.08	11⅝	11.76	10.00
7¾	9.41	7.16	11¾	11.84	10.09
7⅞	9.48	7.25	11⅞	11.92	10.19

Example: $150,000 loan at 7% amortized over 30 years. Annual payment per $1,000 is $6.65, so 150 × 6.65 = $997.50 per month. This is a calculation of principal and interest only. It does not include property taxes, insurance, association dues, or other charges.

APPENDIX B

State-by-State
Foreclosure Guide

STATE	TYPE OF SECURITY MOST COMMONLY USED	FORECLOSURE METHOD	REDEMPTION PERIOD	MISC
Alabama	Mortgage	Power of Sale	12 months	Borrower can reinstate loan within 5 days of sale
Alaska	Deed of Trust	Power of Sale	None	Borrower can reinstate loan up to date of sale so long as a notice of defaulted has not been filed more than 2x in the past
Arizona	Mortgage	Judicial	None	
Arkansas	Deed of Trust	Power of Sale	Within one year	
California	Deed of Trust	Power of Sale	None	
Colorado	Deed of Trust	Power of Sale	75 days	Borrower can cure up to sale date
Connecticut	Mortgage	Strict Foreclosure	None, unless ordered by the court	A strict foreclosure vests title in the lender without a sale. Borrower cannot reinstate the loan. A court may delay the foreclosure for up to six months if the borrower is not making enough money!
Delaware	Mortgage	Judicial	None	
Dist. of Columbia	Deed of Trust	Power of Sale	None	Borrower can reinstate up to 45 days before sale once in two consecutive years
Florida	Mortgage	Judicial	Up to the date the clerk files the certificate of sale	
Georgia	Mortgage	Power of Sale	None	
Hawaii	Mortgage	Power of Sale	None	
Idaho	Deed of Trust	Power of Sale	None	Borrower can cure with 115 days of the filing of the notice of default
Illinois	Mortgage	Judicial	Until the latter of 3 months of entry of judgment or 7 months of service of the foreclosure complaint	Borrower has 90 days from the service of the complaint to reinstate
Indiana	Mortgage	Judicial	None	
Iowa	Mortgage	Judicial	One year	
Kansas	Mortgage	Judicial	3-12 months, depending on the property's equity	
Kentucky	Mortgage & Deed of Trust	Judicial	Up to one year if the sale does not bring at least 2/3 of the property's value	
Louisiana	Mortgage	Judicial	None	
Maine	Mortgage	Judicial	Within one year unless the mortgage agreement provides for less	Borrower can reinstate within 30 days of default
Maryland	Deed of Trust	Power of Sale with court supervision	None stated, although equitable redemption permitted	
Massachusetts	Mortgage	Power of Sale	None	
Michigan	Mortgage	Power of Sale	Varies, but generally 6 months on houses	
Minnesota	Mortgage	Power of Sale	6 to 12 months, depending on equity	
Mississippi	Deed of Trust	Power of Sale	None	Borrower can reinstate up to the date of sale
Missouri	Deed of Trust	Power of Sale	One year if the lender purchases the property at sale	
Montana	Deed of Trust	Judicial	None	
Nebraska	Deed of Trust	Judicial	None	Borrower can reinstate before sale
Nevada	Deed of Trust	Power of Sale	None	Borrower has 35 days from filing of notice of default to reinstate loan
New Hampshire	Mortgage	Power of Sale	None	NH mortgage can also have a strict foreclosure provision
New Jersey	Mortgage	Judicial	6 months after entry of judgment	
New Mexico	Mortgage	Judicial	9 months, but may be as little as 1 month by agreement in writing	
New York	Mortgage	Judicial	None	
North Carolina	Deed of Trust	Power of Sale	None	
North Dakota	Mortgage	Judicial	One year	
Ohio	Mortgage	Judicial	Only up to the date of confirmation of sale	
Oklahoma	Mortgage	Judicial	Only up to the date of confirmation of sale	
Oregon	Deed of Trust	Power of Sale	None	Borrower may reinstate up to 5 days before sale
Pennsylvania	Mortgage	Judicial	None	Borrower may reinstate before the sale, up to 3x in 1 year
Rhode Island	Mortgage	Power of Sale	Up to 3 years by filing a lawsuit	
South Carolina	Mortgage	Judicial	None	
South Dakota	Mortgage	Power of Sale	None	Borrower can make lender go through a judicial foreclosure
Tennessee	Deed of Trust	Power of Sale	Up to 2 years	
Texas	Deed of Trust	Power of Sale	None	Borrower has 20 days from notice of default to reinstate loan
Utah	Deed of Trust	Judicial	6 months	Borrower can reinstate within 3 months of notice of default
Vermont	Mortgage	Strict Foreclosure	None	
Virginia	Deed of Trust	Power of Sale	None	
Washington	Deed of Trust	Power of Sale	None	Borrower can reinstate loan up to 11 days before sale
West Virginia	Deed of Trust	Power of Sale	None if the sale is confirmed by the court	Borrower has 10 days from notice of default to reinstate loan
Wisconsin	Mortgage	Judicial	None	Borrower has until sale date to cure default
Wyoming	Mortgage	Power of Sale	None	

APPENDIX C

Sample Forms

Uniform Residential Loan Application [FNMA Form 1003]
Good Faith Estimate of Settlement Costs
Settlement Statement [HUD-1]
Note [Promissory—FNMA]
California Deed of Trust (Short Form)
Mortgage [Florida—FNMA]
Option to Purchase Real Estate [Buyer-Slanted]
Wrap Around Mortgage [or Deed of Trust] Rider
Installment Land Contract
Subordination Agreement

Uniform Residential Loan Application

This application is designed to be completed by the applicant(s) with the Lender's assistance. Applicants should complete this form as "Borrower" or "Co-Borrower," as applicable. Co-Borrower information must also be provided (and the appropriate box checked) when ☐ the income or assets of a person other than the Borrower (including the Borrower's spouse) will be used as a basis for loan qualification or ☐ the income or assets of the Borrower's spouse or other person who has community property rights pursuant to state law will not be used as a basis for loan qualification, but his or her liabilities must be considered because the spouse or other person has community property rights pursuant to applicable law and Borrower resides in a community property state, the security property is located in a community property state, or the Borrower is relying on other property located in a community property state as a basis for repayment of the loan.

If this is an application for joint credit, Borrower and Co-Borrower each agree that we intend to apply for joint credit (sign below):

Borrower _____   Co-Borrower _____

I. TYPE OF MORTGAGE AND TERMS OF LOAN

Mortgage Applied for:	☐ VA ☐ FHA	☐ Conventional ☐ USDA/Rural Housing Service	☐ Other (explain):	Agency Case Number	Lender Case Number

Amount $	Interest Rate %	No. of Months	Amortization Type:	☐ Fixed Rate ☐ GPM	☐ Other (explain): ☐ ARM (type):

II. PROPERTY INFORMATION AND PURPOSE OF LOAN

Subject Property Address (street, city, state & ZIP)	No. of Units

Legal Description of Subject Property (attach description if necessary)	Year Built

Purpose of Loan	☐ Purchase ☐ Construction ☐ Refinance ☐ Construction-Permanent	☐ Other (explain):	Property will be: ☐ Primary Residence ☐ Secondary Residence ☐ Investment

Complete this line if construction or construction-permanent loan.

Year Lot Acquired	Original Cost $	Amount Existing Liens $	(a) Present Value of Lot $	(b) Cost of Improvements $	Total (a + b) $

Complete this line if this is a refinance loan.

Year Acquired	Original Cost $	Amount Existing Liens $	Purpose of Refinance	Describe Improvements Cost: $	☐ made ☐ to be made

Title will be held in what Name(s)	Manner in which Title will be held	Estate will be held in: ☐ Fee Simple ☐ Leasehold (show expiration date)

Source of Down Payment, Settlement Charges, and/or Subordinate Financing (explain)

III. BORROWER INFORMATION

Borrower	Co-Borrower
Borrower's Name (include Jr. or Sr. if applicable)	Co-Borrower's Name (include Jr. or Sr. if applicable)

Social Security Number	Home Phone (incl. area code)	DOB (mm/dd/yyyy)	Yrs. School	Social Security Number	Home Phone (incl. area code)	DOB (mm/dd/yyyy)	Yrs. School

☐ Married ☐ Unmarried (include ☐ Separated single, divorced, widowed)	Dependents (not listed by Co-Borrower) no. ages	☐ Married ☐ Unmarried (include ☐ Separated single, divorced, widowed)	Dependents (not listed by Borrower) no. ages

Present Address (street, city, state, ZIP) ☐ Own ☐ Rent ___ No. Yrs.	Present Address (street, city, state, ZIP) ☐ Own ☐ Rent ___ No. Yrs.

Mailing Address, if different from Present Address	Mailing Address, if different from Present Address

If residing at present address for less than two years, complete the following:

Former Address (street, city, state, ZIP) ☐ Own ☐ Rent ___ No. Yrs.	Former Address (street, city, state, ZIP) ☐ Own ☐ Rent ___ No. Yrs.

IV. EMPLOYMENT INFORMATION

Borrower	Co-Borrower
Name & Address of Employer ☐ Self Employed	Yrs. on this job	Name & Address of Employer ☐ Self Employed	Yrs. on this job
	Yrs. employed in this line of work/profession		Yrs. employed in this line of work/profession
Position/Title/Type of Business	Business Phone (incl. area code)	Position/Title/Type of Business	Business Phone (incl. area code)

If employed in current position for less than two years or if currently employed in more than one position, complete the following:

Borrower			IV. EMPLOYMENT INFORMATION (cont'd)		Co-Borrower	
Name & Address of Employer	☐ Self Employed	Dates (from – to)	Name & Address of Employer	☐ Self Employed	Dates (from – to)	
		Monthly Income $			Monthly Income $	
Position/Title/Type of Business		Business Phone (incl. area code)	Position/Title/Type of Business		Business Phone (incl. area code)	
Name & Address of Employer	☐ Self Employed	Dates (from – to)	Name & Address of Employer	☐ Self Employed	Dates (from – to)	
		Monthly Income $			Monthly Income $	
Position/Title/Type of Business		Business Phone (incl. area code)	Position/Title/Type of Business		Business Phone (incl. area code)	

V. MONTHLY INCOME AND COMBINED HOUSING EXPENSE INFORMATION

Gross Monthly Income	Borrower	Co-Borrower	Total	Combined Monthly Housing Expense	Present	Proposed
Base Empl. Income*	$	$	$	Rent	$	
Overtime				First Mortgage (P&I)		$
Bonuses				Other Financing (P&I)		
Commissions				Hazard Insurance		
Dividends/Interest				Real Estate Taxes		
Net Rental Income				Mortgage Insurance		
Other (before completing, see the notice in "describe other income," below)				Homeowner Assn. Dues		
				Other:		
Total	$	$	$	Total	$	$

    *****   Self Employed Borrower(s) may be required to provide additional documentation such as tax returns and financial statements.

Describe Other Income   *Notice:* **Alimony, child support, or separate maintenance income need not be revealed if the Borrower (B) or Co-Borrower (C) does not choose to have it considered for repaying this loan.**

B/C		Monthly Amount
		$

VI. ASSETS AND LIABILITIES

This Statement and any applicable supporting schedules may be completed jointly by both married and unmarried Co-Borrowers if their assets and liabilities are sufficiently joined so that the Statement can be meaningfully and fairly presented on a combined basis; otherwise, separate Statements and Schedules are required. If the Co-Borrower section was completed about a non-applicant spouse or other person, this Statement and supporting schedules must be completed about that spouse or other person also.

Completed ☐ Jointly ☐ Not Jointly

ASSETS Description	Cash or Market Value	Liabilities and Pledged Assets. List the creditor's name, address, and account number for all outstanding debts, including automobile loans, revolving charge accounts, real estate loans, alimony, child support, stock pledges, etc. Use continuation sheet, if necessary. Indicate by (*) those liabilities, which will be satisfied upon sale of real estate owned or upon refinancing of the subject property.		
Cash deposit toward purchase held by:	$			
List checking and savings accounts below		**LIABILITIES**	Monthly Payment & Months Left to Pay	Unpaid Balance
Name and address of Bank, S&L, or Credit Union		Name and address of Company	$ Payment/Months	$
Acct. no.	$	Acct. no.		
Name and address of Bank, S&L, or Credit Union		Name and address of Company	$ Payment/Months	$
Acct. no.	$	Acct. no.		
Name and address of Bank, S&L, or Credit Union		Name and address of Company	$ Payment/Months	$
Acct. no.	$	Acct. no.		

VI. ASSETS AND LIABILITIES (cont'd)

Name and address of Bank, S&L, or Credit Union	Name and address of Company	$ Payment/Months	$
Acct. no. $	Acct. no.		
Stocks & Bonds (Company name/ number & description) $	Name and address of Company	$ Payment/Months	$
	Acct. no.		
Life insurance net cash value $	Name and address of Company	$ Payment/Months	$
Face amount: $			
Subtotal Liquid Assets $			
Real estate owned (enter market value from schedule of real estate owned) $			
Vested interest in retirement fund $			
Net worth of business(es) owned (attach financial statement) $	Acct. no.		
Automobiles owned (make and year) $	Alimony/Child Support/Separate Maintenance Payments Owed to:	$	
Other Assets (itemize) $	Job-Related Expense (child care, union dues, etc.)	$	
	Total Monthly Payments	$	
Total Assets a. $	Net Worth (a minus b) ▶ $	**Total Liabilities b.**	$

Schedule of Real Estate Owned (If additional properties are owned, use continuation sheet.)

Property Address (enter S if sold, PS if pending sale or R if rental being held for income) ▼	Type of Property	Present Market Value	Amount of Mortgages & Liens	Gross Rental Income	Mortgage Payments	Insurance, Maintenance, Taxes & Misc.	Net Rental Income
		$	$	$	$	$	$
Totals		$	$	$	$	$	$

List any additional names under which credit has previously been received and indicate appropriate creditor name(s) and account number(s):

Alternate Name	Creditor Name	Account Number

VII. DETAILS OF TRANSACTION

a.	Purchase price	$
b.	Alterations, improvements, repairs	
c.	Land (if acquired separately)	
d.	Refinance (incl. debts to be paid off)	
e.	Estimated prepaid items	
f.	Estimated closing costs	
g.	PMI, MIP, Funding Fee	
h.	Discount (if Borrower will pay)	
i.	Total costs (add items a through h)	

VIII. DECLARATIONS

If you answer "Yes" to any questions a through i, please use continuation sheet for explanation.

	Borrower Yes No	Co-Borrower Yes No
a. Are there any outstanding judgments against you?	☐ ☐	☐ ☐
b. Have you been declared bankrupt within the past 7 years?	☐ ☐	☐ ☐
c. Have you had property foreclosed upon or given title or deed in lieu thereof in the last 7 years?	☐ ☐	☐ ☐
d. Are you a party to a lawsuit?	☐ ☐	☐ ☐
e. Have you directly or indirectly been obligated on any loan which resulted in foreclosure, transfer of title in lieu of foreclosure, or judgment?	☐ ☐	☐ ☐

(This would include such loans as home mortgage loans, SBA loans, home improvement loans, educational loans, manufactured (mobile) home loans, any mortgage, financial obligation, bond, or loan guarantee. If "Yes," provide details, including date, name, and address of Lender, FHA or VA case number, if any, and reasons for the action.)

VII. DETAILS OF TRANSACTION		VIII. DECLARATIONS				
			Borrower		Co-Borrower	
		If you answer "Yes" to any questions a through i, please use continuation sheet for explanation.	Yes	No	Yes	No
j. Subordinate financing						
k. Borrower's closing costs paid by Seller		f. Are you presently delinquent or in default on any Federal debt or any other loan, mortgage, financial obligation, bond, or loan guarantee? If "Yes," give details as described in the preceding question.	☐	☐	☐	☐
l. Other Credits (explain)		g. Are you obligated to pay alimony, child support, or separate maintenance?	☐	☐	☐	☐
		h. Is any part of the down payment borrowed?	☐	☐	☐	☐
m. Loan amount (exclude PMI, MIP, Funding Fee financed)		i. Are you a co-maker or endorser on a note?	☐	☐	☐	☐
		j. Are you a U.S. citizen?	☐	☐	☐	☐
n. PMI, MIP, Funding Fee financed		k. Are you a permanent resident alien?	☐	☐	☐	☐
		l. Do you intend to occupy the property as your primary residence? If "Yes," complete question m below.	☐	☐	☐	☐
o. Loan amount (add m & n)						
		m. Have you had an ownership interest in a property in the last three years?	☐	☐	☐	☐
p. Cash from/to Borrower (subtract j, k, l & o from i)		(1) What type of property did you own—principal residence (PR), second home (SH), or investment property (IP)? (2) How did you hold title to the home—solely by yourself (S), jointly with your spouse (SP), or jointly with another person (O)?		___		___

IX. ACKNOWLEDGEMENT AND AGREEMENT

Each of the undersigned specifically represents to Lender and to Lender's actual or potential agents, brokers, processors, attorneys, insurers, servicers, successors and assigns and agrees and acknowledges that: (1) the information provided in this application is true and correct as of the date set forth opposite my signature and that any intentional or negligent misrepresentation of this information contained in this application may result in civil liability, including monetary damages, to any person who may suffer any loss due to reliance upon any misrepresentation that I have made on this application, and/or in criminal penalties including, but not limited to, fine or imprisonment or both under the provisions of Title 18, United States Code, Sec. 1001, et seq.; (2) the loan requested pursuant to this application (the "Loan") will be secured by a mortgage or deed of trust on the property described in this application; (3) the property will not be used for any illegal or prohibited purpose or use; (4) all statements made in this application are made for the purpose of obtaining a residential mortgage loan; (5) the property will be occupied as indicated in this application; (6) the Lender, its servicers, successors or assigns may retain the original and/or an electronic record of this application, whether or not the Loan is approved; (7) the Lender and its agents, brokers, insurers, servicers, successors, and assigns may continuously rely on the information contained in the application, and I am obligated to amend and/or supplement the information provided in this application if any of the material facts that I have represented herein should change prior to closing of the Loan; (8) in the event that my payments on the Loan become delinquent, the Lender, its servicers, successors or assigns may, in addition to any other rights and remedies that it may have relating to such delinquency, report my name and account information to one or more consumer reporting agencies; (9) ownership of the Loan and/or administration of the Loan account may be transferred with such notice as may be required by law; (10) neither Lender nor its agents, brokers, insurers, servicers, successors or assigns has made any representation or warranty, express or implied, to me regarding the property or the condition or value of the property; and (11) my transmission of this application as an "electronic record" containing my "electronic signature," as those terms are defined in applicable federal and/or state laws (excluding audio and video recordings), or my facsimile transmission of this application containing a facsimile of my signature, shall be as effective, enforceable and valid as if a paper version of this application were delivered containing my original written signature.

Acknowledgement. Each of the undersigned hereby acknowledges that any owner of the Loan, its servicers, successors and assigns, may verify or reverify any information contained in this application or obtain any information or data relating to the Loan, for any legitimate business purpose through any source, including a source named in this application or a consumer reporting agency.

Borrower's Signature	Date	Co-Borrower's Signature	Date
X		X	

X. INFORMATION FOR GOVERNMENT MONITORING PURPOSES

The following information is requested by the Federal Government for certain types of loans related to a dwelling in order to monitor the lender's compliance with equal credit opportunity, fair housing and home mortgage disclosure laws. You are not required to furnish this information, but are encouraged to do so. The law provides that a lender may not discriminate either on the basis of this information, or on whether you choose to furnish it. If you furnish the information, please provide both ethnicity and race. For race, you may check more than one designation. If you do not furnish ethnicity, race, or sex, under Federal regulations, this lender is required to note the information on the basis of visual observation and surname if you have made this application in person. If you do not wish to furnish the information, please check the box below. (Lender must review the above material to assure that the disclosures satisfy all requirements to which the lender is subject under applicable state law for the particular type of loan applied for.)

BORROWER ☐ I do not wish to furnish this information	CO-BORROWER ☐ I do not wish to furnish this information
Ethnicity: ☐ Hispanic or Latino ☐ Not Hispanic or Latino	Ethnicity: ☐ Hispanic or Latino ☐ Not Hispanic or Latino
Race: ☐ American Indian or Alaska Native ☐ Asian ☐ Black or African American ☐ Native Hawaiian or Other Pacific Islander ☐ White	Race: ☐ American Indian or Alaska Native ☐ Asian ☐ Black or African American ☐ Native Hawaiian or Other Pacific Islander ☐ White
Sex: ☐ Female ☐ Male	Sex: ☐ Female ☐ Male

To be Completed by Interviewer This application was taken by: ☐ Face-to-face interview ☐ Mail ☐ Telephone ☐ Internet	Interviewer's Name (print or type)	Name and Address of Interviewer's Employer
	Interviewer's Signature Date	
	Interviewer's Phone Number (incl. area code)	

CONTINUATION SHEET/RESIDENTIAL LOAN APPLICATION		
Use this continuation sheet if you need more space to complete the Residential Loan Application. Mark **B** f or Borrower or **C** for Co-Borrower.	Borrower:	Agency Case Number:
	Co-Borrower:	Lender Case Number:

I/We fully understand that it is a Federal crime punishable by fine or imprisonment, or both, to knowingly make any false statements concerning any of the above facts as applicable under the provisions of Title 18, United States Code, Section 1001, et seq.

Borrower's Signature	Date	Co-Borrower's Signature	Date
X		X	

GOOD FAITH ESTIMATE OF SETTLEMENT COSTS

Lender:
Applicants:

Property Address:

☐ FHA   ☐ V.A.   ☐ CONV.   Est. Rate: Loan Amount: Date:

The information provided below reflects estimates of the charges which you are likely to incur at the settlement of your loan. The fees listed are estimates - actual charges may be more or less. Your transaction may not involve a fee for every item listed.

The numbers listed beside the estimates generally correspond to the numbered lines contained in the HUD-1 settlement statement which you will be receiving at settlement. The HUD-1 settlement statement will show you the actual cost for items paid at settlement.

ESTIMATED SETTLEMENT CHARGES

	Lender Charged	Broker Charged	PAID BY			
			Lender	Broker	Buyer	Seller
801. Loan Origination Fee $:						
802. Discount Points $:						
803. Appraisal Fee $:						
804. Credit Report $:						
805. Lenders Inspection Fee $:						
806. Mortgage Insurance Application Fee $:						
807. Assumption Fee $:						
808. Tax Service Contract $:						
901. Interest for ____days @ $ _____ per day						
902. Mortgage Insurance Premium (PMI/MIP) $:						
903. Hazard Insurance Premium for 1 year $:						
904. Flood Insurance Premium for 1 year $:						
1001. Hazard Ins. ____ mos. @$ _____						
1002. Mortgage Ins. ____ mos. @$ _____						
1003. City Taxes ____ mos. @$ _____						
1004. County Taxes ____ mos. @$ _____						
1006. Flood Ins. ____ mos. @$ _____						
1101. Settlement or Closing Fees $:						
1102. Abstract or Title Search $:						
1103. Title Examination $:						
1104. Title Insurance Binder $:						
1105. Escrow Document Preparation $:						
1106. Notary Fee $:						
1107. Attorneys' Fees $:						
1108. Title Insurance $:						
1201. Recording Fees $:						
1202. City/County Tax Stamps $:						
1203. State Tax Stamps $:						
1204. Assignment Fee $:						
1301. Survey $:						
1302. Termite Inspection $:						
_____ _____						
_____ _____						
			LENDER	**BROKER**	**BUYER**	**SELLER**

TOTAL ESTIMATED FUNDS NEEDED TO CLOSE

These estimates are provided pursuant to the Real Estate Settlment Procedure Act of 1974, as amended (RESPA). Additional information can be found in the HUD Special Information Booklet which is to be provided to you by your mortgage broker or lender. The undersigned acknowledges receipt of the booklet "Settlement Costs," and if applicable the Consumer Handbook on ARM Mortgages.

A. SETTLEMENT STATEMENT	U.S. DEPARTMENT OF HOUSING AND URBAN DEVELOPMENT			OMB No. 2502-0265

B. TYPE OF LOAN

1. ☐ FHA	2. ☐ FmHA	3. ☒ CONV.UNINS.	6. File Number:	7. Loan Number:	8. Mortgage Insurance Case Number:
4. ☐ VA	5. ☐ CONV.INS.				

C. NOTE: This form is furnished to give you a statement of actual settlement costs. Amounts paid to and by the settlement agent are shown. Items marked "(p.o.c)" were paid outside the closing; they are shown here for informational purposes and are not included in the totals.

D. NAME AND ADDRESS OF BORROWER:	E. NAME AND ADDRESS OF SELLER/TAX I.D.:	F. NAME AND ADDRESS OF LENDER:
		Resource Bank 10461 White Granite Drive Oakton, Virginia 22124

G. PROPERTY LOCATION:	H. SETTLEMENT AGENT: NORTH AMERICAN TITLE COMPANY OF COLORADO PLACE OF SETTLEMENT: 6501 E. Belleview Avenue, Suite 130 Englewood, CO 80111	I. SETTLEMENT DATE: 05/14/01

J. SUMMARY OF BORROWER'S TRANSACTION		K. SUMMARY OF SELLER'S TRANSACTION	
100. GROSS AMOUNT DUE FROM BORROWER:		**400. GROSS AMOUNT DUE TO SELLER:**	
101. Contract Sales Price	115,000.00	401. Contract Sales Price	115,000.00
102. Personal property		402. Personal property	
103. Settlement charges to borrower (line 1400)	4,463.00	403.	
104. Add'l Working capital	68.00	404.	
105. HOA dues/ June & July	254.00	405.	
Adjustments for items paid by seller in advance		Adjustments for items paid by seller in advance	
106. City/town taxes to		406. City/town taxes to	
107. County taxes to		407. County taxes to	
108. Assessments to		408. Assessments to	
109.		409.	
110. HOA working capital	186.00	410. HOA working capital	186.00
111.		411.	
112.		412.	
113.		413.	
114.		414.	
120. GROSS AMOUNT DUE FROM BORROWER	119,971.00	**420. GROSS AMOUNT DUE TO SELLER**	115,186.00
200. AMOUNTS PAID BY OR IN BEHALF OF BORROWER:		**500. REDUCTIONS IN AMOUNT DUE TO SELLER:**	
201. Deposit or earnest money	2,000.00	501. Excess deposit (see instructions)	
202. Principal amount of new loan(s)	92,000.00	502. Settlement charges to seller (line 1400)	6,775.26
203. Existing loan(s) taken subject to		503. Existing loan(s) taken subject to	
204.		504. Payoff of first mortgage loan	53,633.00
205.		505. Payoff of second mortgage loan	
206.		506.	
207.		507. HOA statement fee	60.00
208.		508. 2nd half 2000 taxes	256.31
209.		509. Hoa transfer fee	100.00
Adjustments for items unpaid by seller		Adjustments for items unpaid by seller	
210. City/town taxes to		510. City/town taxes to	
211. County taxes 01/01/01 to 05/14/01	186.80	511. County taxes 01/01/01 to 05/14/01	186.80
212. Assessments to		512. Assessments to	
213.		513.	
214.		514.	
215.		515.	
216.		516.	
217.		517.	
218.		518.	
219.		519.	
220. TOTAL PAID BY/FOR BORROWER	94,186.80	**520. TOTAL REDUCTION AMOUNT DUE SELLER**	61,011.37
300. CASH AT SETTLEMENT FROM/TO BORROWER		**600. CASH AT SETTLEMENT TO/FROM SELLER**	
301. Gross amount due from borrower (line 120)	119,971.00	601. Gross amount due to seller (line 420)	115,186.00
302. Less amounts paid by/for borrower (line 220)	94,186.80	602. Less reductions in amount due seller (line 520)	61,011.37
303. CASH (☒ FROM) (☐ TO) BORROWER	25,784.20	603. CASH (☒ TO) (☐ FROM) SELLER	54,174.63

I have carefully reviewed the HUD-1 Settlement Statement and to the best of my knowledge and belief it is a true and accurate statement of all receipts and disbursements made on my account or by me in this transaction. I further certify that I have received a copy of the HUD-1 Settlement Statement.

_____   _____
Borrowers   Sellers

The HUD-1 Settlement Statement which I have prepared is a true and accurate account of this transaction. I have caused or will cause the funds to be disbursed in accordance with this statement.

_____   5/14/01
Settlement Agent   Date

Warning: It is a crime to knowingly make false statements to the United States on this or any similar form.
Penalties upon conviction can include a fine and imprisonment. For details see: Title 18 U.S. Code Section 1001 and Section 1010.

HUD-1 (8-87)
RESPA, HB 4305.2
Previous edition is obsolete.

-2-

L. SETTLEMENT CHARGES	PAID FROM BORROWER'S FUNDS AT SETTLEMENT	PAID FROM SELLER'S FUNDS AT SETTLEMENT
700. TOTAL SALES/BROKER'S COMMISSION		
based on price $ 115,000.00 @ 5.00 %= 5,750.00		
Division of Commission (line 700) as follows:		
701. $ 2,530.00 to Re/Max Classic		
702. $ 3,220.00 to Keller Williams		
703. Commission paid at Settlement		5,750.00
704.		
800. ITEMS PAYABLE IN CONNECTION WITH LOAN		
801. Loan Origination Fee 1.000 % Stonecreek Funding	1,500.00	
802. Loan Discount 0.050 % Resource Bank	460.00	
803. Appraisal Fee to Stonecreek Funding	350.00	
804. Credit Report to Stonecreek Funding	15.00	
805. Lenders Inspection Fee		
806. Mortgage Insurance Application Fee to		
807. Assumption Fee		
808. Tax Service Fee Resource Bank	83.00	
809. doc.prep. fee Resource Bank	275.00	
810. portfolio review Resource Bank	100.00	
811. flood cert. Resource Bank	26.00	
812. underwriting fee Resource Bank	150.00	
813.		
814.		
815.		
816.		
900. ITEMS REQUIRED BY LENDER TO BE PAID IN ADVANCE		
901. Interest from 05/14/01 to 06/01/01 @$ 17.888900 /day	322.00	
902. Mortgage Insurance Premium for months to		
903. Hazard Insurance Premium for years to		
904. Flood Insurance Premium for years to		
905.		
1000. RESERVES DEPOSITED WITH LENDER		
1001. Hazard Insurance months @$ per month		
1002. Mortgage Insurance months @$ per month		
1003. City property taxes months @$ per month		
1004. County property taxes 9 months @$ 42.72 per month	384.48	
1005. Annual assessments months @$ per month		
1006. Flood insurance months @$ per month		
1007. months @$ per month		
1008. Aggregate Adjustment months @$ per month	-42.72	
1100. TITLE CHARGES		
1101. Settlement or closing fee to North American Title Company	75.00	75.00
1102. Abstract or title search to		
1103. Title examination to		
1104. Title insurance binder to		
1105. Document preparation to		
1106. Notary fees to		
1107. Attorney's fees to		
(includes above items numbers:)		
1108. Title insurance to North American Title Company	125.00	852.00
(includes above items numbers:)		
1109. Lender's coverage $ 93,000.00 852.00		
1110. Owner's coverage $ 115,000.00 852.00		
1111. Endorsement Forms 100 & 8.1 North American Title Company	80.00	
1112. End. 115.1 North American Title Company	100.00	
1113. Tax Certificate North American Title Company	30.00	
1114. Loan closing fee North American Title Company	175.00	
1115.		
1200. GOVERNMENT RECORDING AND TRANSFER CHARGES		
1201. Recording fees: Deed $ 5.00 :Mortgage $ 125.00 :Releases $ 25.00	130.00	25.00
1202. State tax/stamps: Deed $:Mortgage $	11.50	
1203. escrow recording Arapahoe Cty Clerk & Recorder	20.00	
1204.		
1205.		
1300. ADDITIONAL SETTLEMENT CHARGES		
1301. Survey to		
1302. Pest inspection to		
1303. HOA dues May Spinnaker Run HOA	73.74	53.26
1304. UPS charges North American Title Company	20.00	20.00
1305.		
1306.		
1307.		
1308.		
1309.		
1310.		
1311.		
1400. TOTAL SETTLEMENT CHARGES(enter on lines 103,Sect J and 502,Sect K)	4,463.00	6,775.26

NOTE

January 15, 2002   Denver   Colorado
[Date]   [City]   [State]

123 Main Street, Denver, CO 80231
[Property Address]

1. BORROWER'S PROMISE TO PAY

In return for a loan that I have received, 1 promise to pay U.S. $ 100,000.00   (this amount is called "principal"), plus interest, to the order of the Lender. The Lender is

ABC Home Loan Mortgage Corporation

. I understand that the Lender may transfer this Note. The Lender or anyone who takes this Note by transfer and who is entitled to receive payments under this Note is called the "Note Holder."

2. INTEREST

Interest will be charged on unpaid principal until the full amount of principal has been paid. I will pay interest at a yearly rate of   10   %.

The interest rate required by this Section 2 is the rate I will pay both before and after any default described in Section 6(B) of this Note.

3. PAYMENTS

(A) Time and Place of Payments

I will pay principal and interest by making payments every month.

I will make my monthly payments on the   First   day of each month beginning on Feb 15   , 2002   . I will make these payments every month until I have paid all of the principal and interest and any other charges described below that I may owe under this Note. My monthly payments will be applied to interest before principal. If, on March 15, 2007   , I still owe amounts under this Note, I will pay those amounts in full on that date, which is called the "Maturity Date."

I will make my monthly payments at PO Box 1234, Denver, CO 80202

or at a different place if required by the Note Holder.

(B) Amount of Monthly Payments

My monthly payment will be in the amount of U.S.$ 112.00   .

4. BORROWER'S RIGHT TO PREPAY

I have the right to make payments of principal at any time before they are due. A payment of principal only is known as a "prepayment." When I make a prepayment, I will tell the Note Holder in writing that I am doing so.

I may make a full prepayment or partial prepayments without paying any prepayment charge. The Note Holder will use all of my prepayments to reduce the amount of principal that I owe under this Note. If I make a partial prepayment, there will be no changes in the due date or in the amount of my monthly payment unless the Note Holder agrees in writing to those changes.

5. LOAN CHARGES

If a law, which applies to this loan and which sets maximum loan charges, is finally interpreted so that the interest or other loan charges collected or to be collected in connection with this loan exceed the permitted limits, then: (i) any such loan charge shall be reduced by the amount necessary to reduce the charge to the permitted limit, and (ii) any sums already collected from me which exceeded permitted limits will be refunded to me. The Note Holder may choose to make this refund by reducing the principal I owe under this Note or by making a direct payment to me. If a refund reduces principal, the reduction will be treated as a partial prepayment.

6. BORROWER'S FAILURE TO PAY AS REQUIRED

(A) Late Charge for Overdue Payments

If the Note Holder has not received the full amount of any monthly payment by the end of   15   calendar days after the date it is due, I will pay a late charge to the Note Holder. The amount of the charge will be   5   % of my overdue payment of principal and interest. I will pay this late charge promptly but only once on each late payment.

(B) Default

If I do not pay the full amount of each monthly payment on the date it is due, I will be in default.

MULTISTATE FIXED RATE NOTE - Single Family - **FNMA/FHLMC Uniform Instrument**

Form 3200 12/83
Amended 5/91

(C) Notice of Default

If I am in default, the Note Holder may send me a written notice telling me that if I do not pay the overdue amount by a certain date, the Note Holder may require me to pay immediately the full amount of principal which has not been paid and all the interest that I owe on that amount. That date must be at least 30 days after the date on which the notice is delivered or mailed to me.

(D) No Waiver by Note Holder

Even if, at a time when I am in default, the Note Holder does not require me to pay immediately in full as described above, the Note Holder will still have the right to do so if I am in default at a later time.

(E) Payment of Note Holder's Costs and Expenses

If the Note Holder has required me to pay immediately in full as described above, the Note Holder will have the right to be paid back by me for all of its costs and expenses in enforcing this Note to the extent not prohibited by applicable law. Those expenses include, for example, reasonable attorneys' fees.

7. GIVING OF NOTICES

Unless applicable law requires a different method, any notice that must be given to me under this Note will be given by delivering it or by mailing it by first class mail to me at the Property Address above or at a different address if I give the Note Holder a notice of my different address.

Any notice that must be given to the Note Holder under this Note will be given by mailing it by first class mail to the Note Holder at the address stated in Section 3(A) above or at a different address if I am given a notice of that different address.

8. OBLIGATIONS OF PERSONS UNDER THIS NOTE

If more than one person signs this Note, each person is fully and personally obligated to keep all of the promises made in this Note, including the promise to pay the full amount owed. Any person who is a guarantor, surety or endorser of this Note is also obligated to do these things. Any person who takes over these obligations, including the obligations of a guarantor, surety or endorser of this Note, is also obligated to keep all of the promises made in this Note. The Note Holder may enforce its rights under this Note against each person individually or against all of us together. This means that any one of us may be required to pay all of the amounts owed under this Note.

9. WAIVERS

I and any other person who has obligations under this Note waive the rights of presentment and notice of dishonor. "Presentment" means the right to require the Note Holder to demand payment of amounts due. "Notice of dishonor" means the right to require the Note Holder to give notice to other persons that amounts due have not been paid.

10. UNIFORM SECURED NOTE

This Note is a uniform instrument with limited variations in some jurisdictions. In addition to the protections given to the Note Holder under this Note, a Mortgage, Deed of Trust or Security Deed (the "Security Instrument"), dated the same date as this Note, protects the Note Holder from possible losses which might result if I do not keep the promises which I make in this Note. That Security Instrument describes how and under what conditions I may be required to make immediate payment in full of all amounts I owe under this Note. Some of those conditions are described as follows:

Transfer of the Property or a Beneficial Interest in Borrower. If all or any part of the Property or any interest in it is sold or transferred (or if a beneficial interest in Borrower is sold or transferred and Borrower is not a natural person), without Lender's prior written consent, Lender may, at its option, require immediate payment in full of all sums secured by this Security Instrument. However, this option shall not be exercised by Lender if exercise is prohibited by federal law as of the date of this Security Instrument.

If Lender exercises this option, Lender shall give Borrower notice of acceleration. The notice shall provide a period of not less than 30 days from the date the notice is delivered or mailed within which Borrower must pay all sums secured by this Security Instrument. If Borrower fails to pay these sums prior to the expiration of this period, Lender may invoke any remedies permitted by this Security Instrument without further notice or demand on Borrower.

WITNESS THE HAND(S) AND SEAL(S) OF THE UNDERSIGNED.

Barney Borrower _____ (Seal)
                                              -Borrower
SSN: _____

_____ (Seal)
          -Borrower
SSN: _____

_____ (Seal)
          -Borrower
SSN: _____

_____ (Seal)
          -Borrower
SSN: _____

[Sign Original Only]

Form 3200 12/83

APPENDIX C

RECORDING REQUESTED BY

AND WHEN RECORDED MAIL TO

CALIFORNIA DEED OF TRUST
(SHORT FORM)

SHORT FORM DEED OF TRUST, executed this   1st   day of   March, 2001   by and between between

Harry Homeowner, an unmarried man   , herein called Trustor,

whose address is   PO Box 12, Los Angeles, CA 90000

California Trust Company   , herein called Trustee, and

ABC Home Loan Corporation   , herein called Beneficiary,

THE TRUSTOR IRREVOCABLY GRANTS, TRANSFERS AND ASSIGNS TO TRUSTEE IN TRUST, WITH POWER OF SALE, that
property located in Los Angeles   County, California, described as:

Lot 12, Block 14, Shady Acres Subdivision, 2nd Filing, City and County of Los Angeles, State of California

Also known as 12345 Bobcat Lane, Los Angeles, CA 90000

TOGETHER WITH the rents, issues and profits thereof, SUBJECT, HOWEVER, to the right, power and authority given to and conferred upon Beneficiary by paragraph (10) of the provisions incorporated herein by reference to collect and apply such rents, issues and profits.
For the Purpose of Securing: 1. Performance of each agreement of Trustor incorporated by reference or contained herein. 2. Payment of the indebtedness evidenced by one promissory note of even date herewith, and any extension or renewal thereof, in the principal sum of $ 100,000.00 _____ executed by Trustor in favor of Beneficiary or order. 3. Payment of such further sums as the then record owner of said property may borrow from Beneficiary, when evidenced by another note (or notes) reciting it is so secured.
    To Protect the Security of This Deed of Trust, Trustor Agrees: By the execution and delivery of this Deed of Trust and the rate secured hereby, that provisions (1) to (14), inclusive, of the fictitious deed of trust recorded October 23, 1961, in the book and at the page of Official Records in the office of the county recorder of the county where said property is located, noted below opposite the name of such county, viz.:

COUNTY	DATE	BOOK	PAGE	COUNTY	DATE	BOOK	PAGE	COUNTY	DATE	BOOK	PAGE	COUNTY	DATE	BOOK	PAGE
IMPERIAL	9/10/68	1267	574	ORANGE	9/6/68	8714	147	SAN BERNARDINO	9/6/98	7090	14	SANTA BARBARA	9/6/68	2244	922
KERN	9/6/68	4195	363	VENTURA	9/6/68	3363	84	SAN LUIS OBISPO	9/6/68	1489	429	LOS ANGELES	8/28/68	T5910	842
RIVERSIDE	9/10/68			ACCOUNT = 87097 YEAR 1968				SAN DIEGO	9/10/68			SERIES 9 BOOK 1968 PAGE 155820			

(which provisions, identical in all counties, are printed on the reverse hereof) hereby are adopted and incorporated herein and made a part hereof as fully as though set forth herein at length; that he will observe and perform said provisions; and that the references to property, obligations, and parties in said provisions shall be construed to refer to the property, obligations, and parties set forth in this Deed of Trust.
    The undersigned Trustor requests that a copy of any Notice of Default and of any Notice of Sale hereunder be mailed to him at his address hereinbefore set forth.

Harry Homeowner
_____   _____
Trustor   Trustor

STATE OF CALIFORNIA
COUNTY OF Los Angeles _____ } SS.

On March 1st , 2002 _____ before me, Nancy Notary _____.
personally   appeared   Harry Homeowner _____
personally known to me (or proved to me on the basis of satisfactory evidence) to be the person(s) whose name(s) is/are subscribed to the within instrument and acknowledged to me that he/she/they executed the same in his/her/their authorized capacity(ies), and that by his/her/their signature(s) on the instrument the person(s), or the entity upon behalf of which the person(s0 acted, executed the instrument.

WITNESS my hand and official seal.   Notary Signature *Nancy Notary* _____

DO NOT RECORD THIS PORTION

The following is a copy of provisions (1) to (14), inclusive, of the fictitious deed of trust, recorded in each county in California, as stated in the foregoing Deed of Trust and incorporated by reference in said Deed of Trust as being a part thereof as if set forth at length therein

To Protect the Security of This Deed of Trust, Trustor Agrees:

(1) To keep said property in good condition and repair, not to remove or demolish any building thereon, to complete or restore promptly and in good and workmanlike manner any building which may be constructed, damaged or destroyed thereon and to pay when due all claims for labor performed and materials furnished therefor, to comply with all laws affecting said property or requiring any alterations or improvements to be made thereon, not to commit or permit waste thereof, not to commit, suffer or permit any act upon said property in violations of law to cultivate, irrigate, fertilize, fumigate, prune and do all other acts which from the character or use of said property may be reasonably necessary, the specific enumerations herein not excluding the general

(2) To provide maintain and deliver to Beneficiary fire insurance satisfactory to and with loss payable to Beneficiary. The amount collected under any fire or other insurance policy may be applied by Beneficiary upon indebtedness secured hereby and in such order as Beneficiary may determine, or at option of Beneficiary the entire amount so collected or any part thereof may be released to Trustor. Such application or release shall not cure or waive any default or notice of default hereunder or invalidate any act done pursuant to such notice

(3) To appear in and defend any action or proceeding purporting to affect the security hereof or the rights or powers of Beneficiary or Trustee, and to pay all costs and expenses including cost of evidence of title and attorney's fees in a reasonable sum, in any such action or proceeding in which Beneficiary or Trustee may appear, and in any suit brought by Beneficiary to foreclose this Deed

(4) To pay at least ten days before delinquency all taxes and assessments affecting said property, including assessments on appurtenant water stock, when due, all encumbrances, charges and liens, with interest, on said property or any part thereof, which appear to be prior or superior hereto, all costs, fees and expenses of this Trust

Should Trustor fail to make any payment or to do any act as herein provided, then Beneficiary or Trustee, but without obligation so to do and without notice to or demand upon Trustor and without releasing Trustor from any obligation hereof, may make or do the same in such manner and to such extent as either may deem necessary to protect the security hereof Beneficiary or Trustee being authorized to enter upon said property for such purposes; appear in and defend any action or proceeding purporting to affect the security hereof or the rights or powers of Beneficiary or Trustee, pay, purchase, contest or compromise any encumbrance, charge or lien which in the judgment of either appears to be prior or superior hereto, and in exercising any such powers, pay necessary expenses, employ counsel and pay his reasonable fees

(5) To pay immediately and without demand all sums so expended by Beneficiary or Trustee, with interest from date of expenditure at the amount allowed by law in effect at the date hereof, and to pay for any statement provided for by law in effect at the date hereof regarding the obligation secured hereby any amount demanded by the Beneficiary not to exceed the maximum allowed by law at the time when said statement is demanded

(6) That any award of damages in connection with any condemnation for public use of or injury to said property or any part thereof is hereby assigned and shall be paid to Beneficiary who may apply or release such moneys received by him in the same manner and with the same effect as above provided for disposition of proceeds of fire or other insurance.

(7) That by accepting payment of any sum secured hereby after its due date, Beneficiary does not waive his rights either to require prompt payment when due of all other sums so secured or to declare default for failure so to pay.

(8) That at any time or from time to time, without liability therefor and without notice, upon written request of Beneficiary and presentation of this Deed and said note for endorsement, and without affecting the personal liability of any person for payment of the indebtedness secured hereby, Trustee may reconvey any part of said property, consent to the making of any map or plot thereof; join in granting any easement thereon; or join in any extension agreement or any agreement subordinating the lien or charge hereof.

(9) That upon written request of Beneficiary state that all sums secured hereby have been paid, and upon surrender of this Deed and said note to Trustee for cancellation and retention and upon payment of its fees, Trustee shall reconvey, without warranty, the property then held hereunder. The recitals in such reconveyance of any matters or facts shall be conclusive proof of the truthfulness thereof. The grantee in such reconveyance may be described as "The person or persons legally entitled thereto "Five years after issuance of such full reconveyance, Trustee may destroy said note and this Deed (unless directed in such request to retain them)

(10) That as additional security, Trustor hereby give to and confers upon Beneficiary the right, power and authority, during the continuance of these Trusts, to collect the rents, issues and profits of said property, reserving unto Trustor the right, prior to any default by Trustor in payment of any indebtedness secured hereby or in performance of any agreement hereunder, to collect the rents, issues and profits of said property, reserving unto Trustor the right, prior to any default by Trustor in payment of any indebtedness secured hereby or in performance of any agreement hereunder, to collect and retain such rents, issues and profits as they become due and payable. Upon any such default, Beneficiary may at any time without notice, either in person , by agent, or by a receiver to be appointed by a court, and without regard to the adequacy of any security for the indebtedness hereby secured, enter upon and take possession of said property or any part thereof, in his own name sue for or otherwise collect such rents, issues and profits, including those past due and unpaid, and apply the same, less costs and expenses of operation and collection, including reasonable attorney's fees. Upon any indebtedness secured hereby, and in such order as Beneficiary may determine. The entering upon and taking possession of said property, the collection of such rents, issues and profits and the application thereof as aforesaid, shall not cure or waive any default or notice of default hereunder or invalidate any act done pursuant to such notice.

(11) That upon default by Trustor in payment of any indebtedness secured hereby or in performance of any agreement hereunder. Beneficiary may declare all sums secured hereby immediately due and payable by delivery to Trustee of written declaration of default and demand for sale and of written notice of default and of election to cause to be sold said property which notice Trustee shall cause to be filed for record. Beneficiary also shall deposit with Trustee this Deed, said note and all documents evidencing expenditures secured hereby .

After the lapse of such time as may then be required by law following the recordation of said notice of default, and notice of sale having been given as then required by law, Trustee, without demand on Trustor, shall sell said property at the time and place fixed by it in said notice of sale, either as a whole or in separate parcels, and in such order as it may determine, at public auction to the highest bidder for cash in lawful money of the United States, payable at time of sale. Trustee may postpone sale of all or any portion of said property by public announcement at such time and place of sale, and from time to time thereafter may postpone such sale by public announcement at the time fixed by the preceding postponement Trustee shall deliver to such purchaser its deed conveying the property so sold, but without any covenant or warranty, express or implied. The recitals in such deed of any matters or facts shall be conclusive proof of the truthfulness thereof. Any person, including Trustor, Trustee, or Beneficiary as hereinafter defined, may purchase at such sale.

After deducting all costs, fees and expenses of Trustee and of this Trust, including cost of evidence of title in connection with sale, Trustee shall apply the proceeds of sale to payment of all sums expended under the terms hereof, not then repaid, with accrued interest at the amount allowed by law in effect at the date hereof, all other sums then secured hereby, and the remainder, if any, to the person or persons legally entitled thereto.

(12) Beneficiary, or any successor in ownership of any indebtedness secured hereby, may from time to time, by instrument in writing, substitute a successor or successors to any Trustee named herein or acting hereunder, which instrument, executed by the Beneficiary and duly acknowledged and recorded in the office of the recorder of the county or counties where said property is situated, shall be conclusive proof of proper substitution of such successor Trustee or Trustees, who shall, without conveyance from the Trustee predecessor, succeed to all its title, estate, rights, powers and duties. Said instrument must contain the name of the original Trustor, Trustee and Beneficiary hereunder, the book and page where this Deed is recorded and the name and address of the new Trustee.

(13) That this Deed applies to, inures to the benefit of, and binds all parties hereto, their heirs, legatees, devisees, administrators, executors, successors and assigns. The term Beneficiary shall mean the owner and holder, including pledgees, of the note secured hereby whether or not named as Beneficiary herein in this Deed, whenever the context so requires, the masculine gender includes the feminine and/or neuter, and the singular number includes the plural.

(14) That Trustee accepts this Trust when this Deed, duly executed and acknowledged, is made a public record as provided by law. Trustee is not obligated to notify any party hereto of pending sale under any other Deed of Trust or of any action or proceeding in which Trustor, Beneficiary or Trustee shall be a party unless brought by Trustee.

After Recording Return To:

_____

_____

_____

_____

-------------------------[Space Above This Line For Recording Data]-------------------------

MORGTAGE

DEFINITIONS

Words used in multiple sections of this document are defined below and other words are defined in Sections 3, 11, 13, 18, 20 and 21. Certain rules regarding the usage of words used in this document are also provided in Section 16.

(A) "Security Instrument" means this document, which is dated _March 1, 2001_ , _____, together with all Riders to this document.

(B) "Borrower" is _Harry Homeowner_ _____. Borrower is the trustor under this Security Instrument.

(C) "Lender" is _ABC Home Loan Corporation_ _____. Lender is a _____ organized and existing under the laws of _Florida_ _____. Lender's address is _PO BOX 322, Miami, FL 38473_ _____. Lender is the beneficiary under this Security Instrument.

(D) "Note" means the promissory note signed by Borrower and dated _March 1, 2001_ , _____. The Note states that Borrower owes Lender _One hundred seventy thousand_ Dollars (U.S. $_$170,000.00_) plus interest. Borrower has promised to pay this debt in regular Periodic Payments and to pay the debt in full not later than_____.

(E) "Property" means the property that is described below under the heading "Transfer of Rights in the Property."

(F) "Loan" means the debt evidenced by the Note, plus interest, any prepayment charges and late charges due under the Note, and all sums due under this Security Instrument, plus interest.

(G) "Riders" means all riders to this Security Instrument that are executed by Borrower. The following riders are to be executed by Borrower [check box as applicable]:

☐ Adjustable Rate Rider   ☐ Condominium Rider   ☐ Second Home Rider
☐ Balloon Rider   ☐ Planned Unit Development Rider ☐ Other(s) [specify] _____
☐ 1-4 Family Rider   ☐ Biweekly Payment Rider   _____

(H) "Applicable Law" means all controlling applicable federal, state and local statutes, regulations, ordinances and administrative rules and orders (that have the effect of law) as well as all applicable final, non-appealable judicial opinions.

(I) "Community Association Dues, Fees and Assessments" means all dues, fees, assessments and other charges that are imposed on Borrower or the Property by a condominium association, homeowners association or similar organization.

(J) "Electronic Funds Transfer" means any transfer of funds, other than a transaction originated by check, draft, or similar paper instrument, which is initiated through an electronic terminal, telephonic instrument, computer, or magnetic tape so as to order, instruct, or authorize a financial institution to debit or credit an account. Such term includes, but is not limited to, point-of-sale transfers, automated teller machine transactions, transfers initiated by telephone, wire transfers, and automated clearinghouse transfers.

(K) "Escrow Items" means those items that are described in Section 3.

(L) "Miscellaneous Proceeds" means any compensation, settlement, award of damages, or proceeds paid by any third party (other than insurance proceeds paid under the coverages described in Section 5) for: (i) damage to, or destruction of, the Property; (ii) condemnation or other taking of all or any part of the Property; (iii) conveyance in lieu of condemnation; or (iv) misrepresentations of, or omissions as to, the value and/or condition of the Property.

(M) "Mortgage Insurance" means insurance protecting Lender against the nonpayment of, or default on, the Loan.

(N) "Periodic Payment" means the regularly scheduled amount due for (i) principal and interest under the Note, plus (ii) any amounts under Section 3 of this Security Instrument.

(O) "RESPA" means the Real Estate Settlement Procedures Act (12 U.S.C. §2601 et seq.) and its implementing regulation, Regulation X (24 C.F.R. Part 3500), as they might be amended from time to time, or any additional or successor legislation or regulation that governs the same subject matter.

As used in this Security Instrument, "RESPA" refers to all requirements and restrictions that are imposed in regard to a "federally related mortgage loan" even if the Loan does not qualify as a "federally related mortgage loan" under RESPA.

(P) "Successor in Interest of Borrower" means any party that has taken title to the Property, whether or not that party has assumed Borrower's obligations under the Note and/or this Security Instrument.

TRANSFER OF RIGHTS IN THE PROPERTY
This Security Instrument secures to Lender: (i) the repayment of the Loan, and all renewals, extensions and modifications of the Note; and (ii) the performance of Borrower's covenants and agreements under this Security Instrument and the Note. For this purpose, Borrower irrevocably

County   Pinellas

_____ of _____ :

[Type of Recording Jurisdiction]   [Name of Recording Jurisdiction]

Lots 8 and 9, Block 35, Orange Subdivision

which currently has the address of 1245 Orange Blossom Way
_____

                                             [Street]

Alligator Alley   FL 33333

_____, _____ ("Property Address"):

[City]   [State, Zip Code]

TOGETHER WITH all the improvements now or hereafter erected on the property, and all easements, appurtenances, and fixtures now or hereafter a part of the property. All replacements and additions shall also be covered by this Security Instrument. All of the foregoing is referred to in this Security Instrument as the "Property."

BORROWER COVENANTS that Borrower is lawfully seised of the estate hereby conveyed and has the right to mortgage, grant and convey the Property and that the Property is unencumbered, except for encumbrances of record. Borrower warrants and will defend generally the title to the Property against all claims and demands, subject to any encumbrances of record.

THIS SECURITY INSTRUMENT combines uniform covenants for national use and non-uniform covenants with limited variations by jurisdiction to constitute a uniform security instrument covering real property.

UNIFORM COVENANTS. Borrower and Lender covenant and agree as follows:

1. Payment of Principal, Interest, Escrow Items, Prepayment Charges, and Late Charges. Borrower shall pay when due the principal of, and interest on, the debt evidenced by the Note and any prepayment charges and late charges due under the Note. Borrower shall also pay funds for Escrow Items pursuant to Section 3. Payments due under the Note and this Security Instrument shall be made in U.S. currency. However, if any check or other instrument received by Lender as payment under the Note or this Security Instrument is returned to Lender unpaid, Lender may require that any or all subsequent payments due under the Note and this Security Instrument be made in one or more of the following forms, as selected by Lender: (a) cash; (b) money order; (c) certified check, bank check, treasurer's check or cashier's check, provided any such check is drawn upon an institution whose deposits are insured by a federal agency, instrumentality, or entity; or (d) Electronic Funds Transfer.

Payments are deemed received by Lender when received at the location designated in the Note or at such other location as may be designated by Lender in accordance with the notice provisions in Section 15. Lender may return any payment or partial payment if the payment or partial payments are insufficient to bring the Loan current. Lender may accept any payment or partial payment insufficient to bring the Loan current, without waiver of any rights hereunder or prejudice to its rights to refuse such payment or partial payments in the future, but Lender is not obligated to apply such payments at the time such payments are accepted. If each Periodic Payment is applied as of its scheduled due date, then Lender need not pay interest on unapplied funds. Lender may hold such unapplied funds until Borrower makes payment to bring the Loan current. If Borrower does not do so within a reasonable period of time, Lender shall either apply such funds or return them to Borrower. If not applied earlier, such funds will be applied to the outstanding principal balance under the Note immediately prior to foreclosure. No offset or claim which Borrower might have now or in the future against Lender shall relieve Borrower from making payments due under the Note and this Security Instrument or performing the covenants and agreements secured by this Security Instrument.

2. Application of Payments or Proceeds. Except as otherwise described in this Section 2, all payments accepted and applied by Lender shall be applied in the following order of priority: (a) interest due under the Note; (b) principal due under the Note; (c) amounts due under Section 3.

Such payments shall be applied to each Periodic Payment in the order in which it became due. Any remaining amounts shall be applied first to late charges, second to any other amounts due under this Security Instrument, and then to reduce the principal balance of the Note.

If Lender receives a payment from Borrower for a delinquent Periodic Payment which includes a sufficient amount to pay any late charge due, the payment may be applied to the delinquent payment and the late charge. If more than one Periodic Payment is outstanding, Lender may apply any payment received from Borrower to the repayment of the Periodic Payments if, and to the extent that, each payment can be paid in full. To the extent that any excess exists after the payment is applied to the full payment of one or more Periodic Payments, such excess may be applied to any late charges due. Voluntary prepayments shall be applied first to any prepayment charges and then as described in the Note.

Any application of payments, insurance proceeds, or Miscellaneous Proceeds to principal due under the Note shall not extend or postpone the due date, or change the amount, of the Periodic Payments.

3. Funds for Escrow Items. Borrower shall pay to Lender on the day Periodic Payments are due under the Note, until the Note is paid in full, a sum (the "Funds") to provide for payment of amounts due for: (a) taxes and assessments and other items which can attain priority over this Security Instrument as a lien or encumbrance on the Property; (b) leasehold payments or ground rents on the Property, if any; (c) premiums for any and all insurance required by Lender under Section 5; and (d) Mortgage Insurance premiums, if any, or any sums payable by Borrower to Lender in lieu of the payment of Mortgage Insurance premiums in accordance with the provisions of Section 10. These items are called "Escrow Items." At origination or at any time during the term of the Loan, Lender may require that Community Association Dues, Fees and Assessments, if any, be escrowed by Borrower, and such dues, fees and assessments shall be an Escrow Item. Borrower shall promptly furnish to Lender all notices of amounts to be paid under this Section. Borrower shall pay Lender the Funds for Escrow Items unless Lender waives Borrower's obligation to pay the Funds for any or all Escrow Items. Lender may waive Borrower's obligation to pay to Lender Funds for any or all Escrow Items at any time. Any such waiver may only be in writing. In the event of such waiver, Borrower shall pay directly, when and where payable, the amounts due for any Escrow Items for which payment of Funds has been waived by Lender and, if Lender requires, shall furnish to Lender receipts evidencing such payment within such time period as Lender may require.

Borrower's obligation to make such payments and to provide receipts shall for all purposes be deemed to be a covenant and agreement contained in this Security Instrument, as the phrase "covenant and agreement" is used in Section 9. If Borrower is obligated to pay Escrow Items directly, pursuant to a waiver, and Borrower fails to pay the amount due for an Escrow Item, Lender may exercise its rights under Section 9 and pay such amount and Borrower shall then be obligated under Section 9 to repay to Lender any such amount. Lender may revoke the waiver as to any or all Escrow Items at any time by a notice given in accordance with Section 15 and, upon such revocation, Borrower shall pay to Lender all Funds, and in such amounts, that are then required under this Section 3.

Lender may, at any time, collect and hold Funds in an amount (a) sufficient to permit Lender to apply the Funds at the time specified under RESPA, and (b) not to exceed the maximum amount a lender can require under RESPA. Lender shall estimate the amount of Funds due on the basis of current data and reasonable estimates of expenditures of future Escrow Items or otherwise in accordance with Applicable Law.

The Funds shall be held in an institution whose deposits are insured by a federal agency, instrumentality, or entity (including Lender, if Lender is an institution whose deposits are so insured) or in any Federal Home Loan Bank. Lender shall apply the Funds to pay the Escrow Items no later than the time specified under RESPA. Lender shall not charge Borrower for holding and applying the Funds, annually analyzing the escrow account, or verifying the Escrow Items, unless Lender pays Borrower interest on the Funds and Applicable Law permits Lender to make such a charge. Unless an agreement is made in writing or Applicable Law requires interest to be paid on the Funds, Lender shall not be required to pay Borrower any interest or earnings on the Funds. Borrower and Lender can agree in writing, however, that interest shall be paid on the Funds. Lender shall give to Borrower, without charge, an annual accounting of the Funds as required by RESPA.

If there is a surplus of Funds held in escrow, as defined under RESPA, Lender shall account to Borrower for the excess funds in accordance with RESPA. If there is a shortage of Funds held in escrow, as defined under RESPA, Lender shall notify Borrower as required by RESPA, and Borrower shall pay to Lender the amount necessary to make up the shortage in accordance with RESPA, but in no more than twelve monthly payments. If there is a deficiency of Funds held in escrow, as defined under RESPA, Lender shall notify Borrower as required by RESPA, and Borrower shall pay to Lender the amount necessary to make up the deficiency in accordance with RESPA, but in no more than twelve monthly payments.

Upon payment in full of all sums secured by this Security Instrument, Lender shall promptly refund to Borrower any Funds held by Lender.

4. Charges; Liens. Borrower shall pay all taxes, assessments, charges, fines, and impositions attributable to the Property which can attain priority over this Security Instrument, leasehold payments or ground rents on the Property, if any, and Community Association Dues, Fees, and Assessments, if any. To the extent that these items are Escrow Items, Borrower shall pay them in the manner provided in Section 3.

Borrower shall promptly discharge any lien which has priority over this Security Instrument unless Borrower: (a) agrees in writing to the payment of the obligation secured by the lien in a manner acceptable to Lender, but only so long as Borrower is performing such agreement; (b) contests the lien in good faith by, or defends against enforcement of the lien in, legal proceedings which in Lender's opinion operate to prevent the enforcement of the lien while those proceedings are pending, but only until such proceedings are concluded; or (c) secures from the holder of the lien an agreement satisfactory to Lender subordinating the lien to this Security Instrument. If Lender determines that any part of the Property is subject to a lien which can attain priority over this Security Instrument, Lender may give Borrower a notice identifying the lien. Within 10 days of the date on which that notice is given, Borrower shall satisfy the lien or take one or more of the actions set forth above in this Section 4.

Lender may require Borrower to pay a one time charge for a real estate tax verification and/or reporting service used by Lender in connection with this Loan.

5. Property Insurance. Borrower shall keep the improvements now existing or hereafter erected on the Property insured against loss by fire, hazards included within the term "extended coverage," and any other hazards including, but not limited to, earthquakes and floods, for which Lender requires insurance. This insurance shall be maintained in the amounts (including deductible levels) and for the periods that Lender requires. What Lender requires pursuant to the preceding sentences can change during the term of the Loan. The insurance carrier providing the insurance shall be chosen by Borrower subject to Lender's right to disapprove Borrower's choice, which right shall not be exercised unreasonably. Lender may require Borrower to pay, in connection with this Loan, either: (a) a one-time charge for flood zone determination, certification and tracking services; or (b) a one-time charge for flood zone determination and certification services and subsequent charges each time remappings or similar changes occur which reasonably might affect such determination or certification. Borrower shall also be responsible for the payment of any fees imposed by the Federal Emergency Management Agency in connection with the review of any flood zone determination resulting from an objection by Borrower.

If Borrower fails to maintain any of the coverages described above, Lender may obtain insurance coverage, at Lender's option and Borrower's expense. Lender is under no obligation to purchase any particular type or amount of coverage. Therefore, such coverage shall cover Lender, but might or might not protect Borrower, Borrower's equity in the Property, or the contents of the Property, against any risk, hazard or liability and might provide greater or lesser coverage than was previously in effect. Borrower acknowledges that the cost of the insurance coverage so obtained might significantly exceed the cost of insurance that Borrower could have obtained. Any amounts disbursed by Lender under this Section 5 shall become additional debt of Borrower secured by this Security Instrument. These amounts shall bear interest at the Note rate from the date of disbursement and shall be payable, with such interest, upon notice from Lender to Borrower requesting payment.

All insurance policies required by Lender and renewals of such policies shall be subject to Lender's right to disapprove such policies, shall include a standard mortgage clause, and shall name Lender as mortgagee and/or as an additional loss payee. Lender shall have the right to hold the policies and renewal certificates. If Lender requires, Borrower shall promptly give to Lender all receipts of paid premiums and renewal notices. If Borrower obtains any form of insurance coverage, not otherwise required by Lender, for damage to, or destruction of, the Property, such policy shall include a standard mortgage clause and shall name Lender as mortgagee and/or as an additional loss payee.

In the event of loss, Borrower shall give prompt notice to the insurance carrier and Lender. Lender may make proof of loss if not made promptly by Borrower. Unless Lender and Borrower otherwise agree in writing, any insurance proceeds, whether or not the underlying insurance was required by Lender, shall be applied to restoration or repair of the Property, if the restoration or repair is economically feasible and Lender's security is not lessened. During such repair and restoration period, Lender shall have the right to hold such insurance proceeds until Lender has had an opportunity to inspect such Property to ensure the work has been completed to Lender's satisfaction, provided that such inspection shall be undertaken promptly. Lender may disburse proceeds for the repairs and restoration in a single payment or in a series of progress payments as the work is completed. Unless an agreement is made in writing or Applicable Law requires interest to be paid on such insurance proceeds, Lender shall not be required to pay Borrower any interest or earnings on such proceeds. Fees for public adjusters, or other third parties, retained by Borrower shall not be paid out of the insurance proceeds and shall be the sole obligation of Borrower. If the restoration or repair is not economically feasible or Lender's security would be lessened, the insurance proceeds shall be applied to the sums secured by this Security Instrument, whether or not then due, with the excess, if any, paid to Borrower. Such insurance proceeds shall be applied in the order provided for in Section 2.

If Borrower abandons the Property, Lender may file, negotiate and settle any available insurance claim and related matters. If Borrower does not respond within 30 days to a notice from Lender that the insurance carrier has offered to settle a claim, then Lender may negotiate and settle the claim. The 30-day period will begin when the notice is given. In either event, or if Lender acquires the Property under Section 22 or otherwise, Borrower hereby assigns to Lender (a) Borrower's rights to any insurance proceeds in an amount not to exceed the amounts unpaid under the Note or this Security Instrument, and (b) any other of Borrower's rights (other than the right to any refund of unearned premiums paid by Borrower) under all insurance policies covering the Property, insofar as such rights are applicable to the coverage of the Property. Lender may use the insurance proceeds either to repair or restore the Property or to pay amounts unpaid under the Note or this Security Instrument, whether or not then due.

6. Occupancy. Borrower shall occupy, establish, and use the Property as Borrower's principal residence within sixty days after the execution of this Security Instrument and shall continue to occupy the Property as Borrower's principal residence for at least one year after the date of occupancy, unless Lender otherwise agrees in writing, which consent shall not be unreasonably withheld, or unless extenuating circumstances exist which are beyond Borrower's control.

7. Preservation, Maintenance and Protection of the Property; Inspections. Borrower shall not destroy, damage or impair the Property, allow the Property to deteriorate or commit waste on the Property. Whether or not Borrower is residing in the Property, Borrower shall maintain the Property in order to prevent the Property from deteriorating or decreasing in value due to its condition. Unless it is determined pursuant to Section 5 that repair or restoration is not economically feasible, Borrower shall promptly repair the Property if damaged to avoid further deterioration or damage. If insurance or condemnation proceeds are paid in connection with damage to, or the taking of, the Property, Borrower shall be responsible for repairing or restoring the Property only if Lender has released proceeds for such purposes. Lender may disburse proceeds for the repairs and restoration in a single payment or in a series of progress payments as the work is completed. If the insurance or condemnation proceeds are not sufficient to repair or restore the Property, Borrower is not relieved of Borrower's obligation for the completion of such repair or restoration.

Lender or its agent may make reasonable entries upon and inspections of the Property. If it has reasonable cause, Lender may inspect the interior of the improvements on the Property. Lender shall give Borrower notice at the time of or prior to such an interior inspection specifying such reasonable cause.

8. Borrower's Loan Application. Borrower shall be in default if, during the Loan application process, Borrower or any persons or entities acting at the direction of Borrower or with Borrower's knowledge or consent gave materially false, misleading, or inaccurate information or statements to Lender (or failed to provide Lender with material information) in connection with the Loan. Material representations include, but are not limited to, representations concerning Borrower's occupancy of the Property as Borrower's principal residence.

9. Protection of Lender's Interest in the Property and Rights Under this Security Instrument. If (a) Borrower fails to perform the covenants and agreements contained in this Security Instrument, (b) there is a legal proceeding that might significantly affect Lender's interest in the Property and/or rights under this Security Instrument (such as a proceeding in bankruptcy, probate, for condemnation or forfeiture, for enforcement of a lien which may attain priority over this Security Instrument or to enforce laws or regulations), or (c) Borrower has abandoned the Property, then Lender may do and pay for whatever is reasonable or appropriate to protect Lender's interest in the Property and rights under this Security Instrument, including protecting and/or assessing the value of the Property, and securing and/or repairing the Property. Lender's actions can include, but are not limited to: (a) paying any sums secured by a lien which has priority over this Security Instrument; (b) appearing in court; and (c) paying reasonable attorneys' fees to protect its interest in the Property and/or rights under this Security Instrument, including its secured position in a bankruptcy proceeding. Securing the Property includes, but is not limited to, entering the Property to make repairs, change locks, replace or board up doors and windows, drain water from pipes, eliminate building or other code violations or dangerous conditions, and have utilities turned on or off. Although Lender may take action under this Section 9, Lender does not have to do so and is not under any duty or obligation to do so. It is agreed that Lender incurs no liability for not taking any or all actions authorized under this Section 9.

Any amounts disbursed by Lender under this Section 9 shall become additional debt of

Borrower secured by this Security Instrument. These amounts shall bear interest at the Note rate from the date of disbursement and shall be payable, with such interest, upon notice from Lender to Borrower requesting payment.

f this Security Instrument is on a leasehold, Borrower shall comply with all the provisions of the lease. If Borrower acquires fee title to the Property, the leasehold and the fee title shall not merge unless Lender agrees to the merger in writing.

10. Mortgage Insurance. If Lender required Mortgage Insurance as a condition of making the Loan, Borrower shall pay the premiums required to maintain the Mortgage Insurance in effect. If, for any reason, the Mortgage Insurance coverage required by Lender ceases to be available from the mortgage insurer that previously provided such insurance and Borrower was required to make separately designated payments toward the premiums for Mortgage Insurance, Borrower shall pay the premiums required to obtain coverage substantially equivalent to the Mortgage Insurance previously in effect, at a cost substantially equivalent to the cost to Borrower of the Mortgage Insurance previously in effect, from an alternate mortgage insurer selected by Lender. If substantially equivalent Mortgage Insurance coverage is not available, Borrower shall continue to pay to Lender the amount of the separately designated payments that were due when the insurance coverage ceased to be in effect. Lender will accept, use and retain these payments as a non-refundable loss reserve in lieu of Mortgage Insurance. Such loss reserve shall be non-refundable, notwithstanding the fact that the Loan is ultimately paid in full, and Lender shall not be required to pay Borrower any interest or earnings on such loss reserve. Lender can no longer require loss reserve payments if Mortgage Insurance coverage (in the amount and for the period that Lender requires) provided by an insurer selected by Lender again becomes available, is obtained, and Lender requires separately designated payments toward the premiums for Mortgage Insurance. If Lender required Mortgage Insurance as a condition of making the Loan and Borrower was required to make separately designated payments toward the premiums for Mortgage Insurance, Borrower shall pay the premiums required to maintain Mortgage Insurance in effect, or to provide a non-refundable loss reserve, until the Lender's requirement for Mortgage Insurance ends in accordance with any` written agreement between Borrower and Lender providing for such termination or until termination is required by Applicable Law. Nothing in this Section 10 affects Borrower's obligation to pay interest at the rate provided in the Note.

11. Assignment of Miscellaneous Proceeds; Forfeiture. All Miscellaneous Proceeds are hereby assigned to and shall be paid to Lender.

If the Property is damaged, such Miscellaneous Proceeds shall be applied to restoration or repair of the Property, if the restoration or repair is economically feasible and Lender's security is not lessened. During such repair and restoration period, Lender shall have the right to hold such Miscellaneous Proceeds until Lender has had an opportunity to inspect such Property to ensure the work has been completed to Lender's satisfaction, provided that such inspection shall be undertaken promptly. Lender may pay for the repairs and restoration in a single disbursement or in a series of progress payments as the work is completed. Unless an agreement is made in writing or Applicable Law requires interest to be paid on such Miscellaneous Proceeds, Lender shall not be required to pay Borrower any interest or earnings on such Miscellaneous Proceeds. If the restoration or repair is not economically feasible or Lender's security would be lessened, the

Miscellaneous Proceeds shall be applied to the sums secured by this Security Instrument, whether or not then due, with the excess, if any, paid to Borrower. Such Miscellaneous Proceeds shall be applied in the order provided for in Section 2.

In the event of a total taking, destruction, or loss in value of the Property, the Miscellaneous Proceeds shall be applied to the sums secured by this Security Instrument, whether or not then due, with the excess, if any, paid to Borrower.

In the event of a partial taking, destruction, or loss in value of the Property in which the fair market value of the Property immediately before the partial taking, destruction, or loss in value is equal to or greater than the amount of the sums secured by this Security Instrument immediately before the partial taking, destruction, or loss in value, unless Borrower and Lender otherwise agree in writing, the sums secured by this Security Instrument shall be reduced by the amount of the Miscellaneous Proceeds multiplied by the following fraction: (a) the total amount of the sums secured immediately before the partial taking, destruction, or loss in value divided by (b) the fair market value of the Property immediately before the partial taking, destruction, or loss in value. Any balance shall be paid to Borrower.

In the event of a partial taking, destruction, or loss in value of the Property in which the fair market value of the Property immediately before the partial taking, destruction, or loss in value is less than the amount of the sums secured immediately before the partial taking, destruction, or loss in value, unless Borrower and Lender otherwise agree in writing, the Miscellaneous Proceeds shall be applied to the sums secured by this Security Instrument whether or not the sums are then due.

If the Property is abandoned by Borrower, or if, after notice by Lender to Borrower that the Opposing Party (as defined in the next sentence) offers to make an award to settle a claim for damages, Borrower fails to respond to Lender within 30 days after the date the notice is given, Lender is authorized to collect and apply the Miscellaneous Proceeds either to restoration or repair of the Property or to the sums secured by this Security Instrument, whether or not then due. "Opposing Party" means the third party that owes Borrower Miscellaneous Proceeds or the party against whom Borrower has a right of action in regard to Miscellaneous Proceeds.
Borrower shall be in default if any action or proceeding, whether civil or criminal, is begun that, in Lender's judgment, could result in forfeiture of the Property or other material impairment of Lender's interest in the Property or rights under this Security Instrument. Borrower can cure such a default and, if acceleration has occurred, reinstate as provided in Section 19, by causing the action or proceeding to be dismissed with a ruling that, in Lender's judgment, precludes forfeiture of the Property or other material impairment of Lender's interest in the Property or rights under this Security Instrument. The proceeds of any award or claim for damages that are attributable to the impairment of Lender's interest in the Property are hereby assigned and shall be paid to Lender.

All Miscellaneous Proceeds that are not applied to restoration or repair of the Property shall be applied in the order provided for in Section 2.

12. Borrower Not Released; Forbearance By Lender Not a Waiver. Extension of the time for payment or modification of amortization of the sums secured by this Security Instrument granted by Lender to Borrower or any Successor in Interest of Borrower shall not operate to release the liability of Borrower or any Successors in Interest of Borrower. Lender shall not be required to commence proceedings against any Successor in Interest of Borrower or to refuse to extend time for payment or otherwise modify amortization of the sums secured by this Security Instrument by reason of any demand made by the original Borrower or any Successors in Interest of Borrower. Any forbearance by Lender in exercising any right or remedy including, without limitation, Lender's acceptance of payments from third persons, entities or Successors in Interest of Borrower or in amounts less than the amount then due, shall not be a waiver of or preclude the exercise of any right or remedy.

13. Joint and Several Liability; Co-signers; Successors and Assigns Bound. Borrower covenants and agrees that Borrower's obligations and liability shall be joint and several. However, any Borrower who co-signs this Security Instrument but does not execute the Note (a "co-signer"): (a) is co-signing this Security Instrument only to mortgage, grant and convey the co-signer's interest in the Property under the terms of this Security Instrument; (b) is not personally obligated to pay the sums secured by this Security Instrument; and (c) agrees that Lender and any other Borrower can agree to extend, modify, forbear or make any accommodations with regard to the terms of this Security Instrument or the Note without the co-signer's consent.

Subject to the provisions of Section 18, any Successor in Interest of Borrower who assumes Borrower's obligations under this Security Instrument in writing, and is approved by Lender, shall obtain all of Borrower's rights and benefits under this Security Instrument. Borrower shall not be released from Borrower's obligations and liability under this Security Instrument unless Lender agrees to such release in writing. The covenants and agreements of this Security Instrument shall bind (except as provided in Section 20) and benefit the successors and assigns of Lender.

14. Loan Charges. Lender may charge Borrower fees for services performed in connection with Borrower's default, for the purpose of protecting Lender's interest in the Property and rights under this Security Instrument, including, but not limited to, attorneys' fees, property inspection and valuation fees. In regard to any other fees, the absence of express authority in this Security Instrument to charge a specific fee to Borrower shall not be construed as a prohibition on the charging of such fee. Lender may not charge fees that are expressly prohibited by this Security Instrument or by Applicable Law.

If the Loan is subject to a law which sets maximum loan charges, and that law is finally interpreted so that the interest or other loan charges collected or to be collected in connection with the Loan exceed the permitted limits, then: (a) any such loan charge shall be reduced by the amount necessary to reduce the charge to the permitted limit; and (b) any sums already collected from Borrower which exceeded permitted limits will be refunded to Borrower. Lender may choose to make this refund by reducing the principal owed under the Note or by making a direct payment to Borrower. If a refund reduces principal, the reduction will be treated as a partial prepayment without any prepayment charge (whether or not a prepayment charge is provided for under the Note).

Borrower's acceptance of any such refund made by direct payment to Borrower will constitute a waiver of any right of action Borrower might have arising out of such overcharge.

15. Notices. All notices given by Borrower or Lender in connection with this Security

Instrument must be in writing. Any notice to Borrower in connection with this Security Instrument shall be deemed to have been given to Borrower when mailed by first class mail or when actually delivered to Borrower's notice address if sent by other means. Notice to any one Borrower shall constitute notice to all Borrowers unless Applicable Law expressly requires otherwise. The notice address shall be the Property Address unless Borrower has designated a substitute notice address by notice to Lender. Borrower shall promptly notify Lender of Borrower's change of address. If Lender specifies a procedure for reporting Borrower's change of address, then Borrower shall only report a change of address through that specified procedure. There may be only one designated notice address under this Security Instrument at any one time. Any notice to Lender shall be given by delivering it or by mailing it by first class mail to Lender's address stated herein unless Lender has designated another address by notice to Borrower. Any notice in connection with this Security Instrument shall not be deemed to have been given to Lender until actually received by Lender. If any notice required by this Security Instrument is also required under Applicable Law, the Applicable Law requirement will satisfy the corresponding requirement under this Security Instrument.

16. Governing Law; Severability; Rules of Construction. This Security Instrument shall be governed by federal law and the law of the jurisdiction in which the Property is located. All rights and obligations contained in this Security Instrument are subject to any requirements and limitations of Applicable Law. Applicable Law might explicitly or implicitly allow the parties to agree by contract or it might be silent, but such silence shall not be construed as a prohibition against agreement by contract. In the event that any provision or clause of this Security Instrument or the Note conflicts with Applicable Law, such conflict shall not affect other provisions of this Security Instrument or the Note which can be given effect without the conflicting provision.

As used in this Security Instrument: (a) words of the masculine gender shall mean and include corresponding neuter words or words of the feminine gender; (b) words in the singular shall mean and include the plural and vice versa; and (c) the word "may" gives sole discretion without any obligation to take any action.

17. Borrower's Copy. Borrower shall be given one copy of the Note and of this Security Instrument.

18. Transfer of the Property or a Beneficial Interest in Borrower. As used in this Section 18, "Interest in the Property" means any legal or beneficial interest in the Property, including, but not limited to, those beneficial interests transferred in a bond for deed, contract for deed, installment sales contract or escrow agreement, the intent of which is the transfer of title by Borrower at a future date to a purchaser.

If all or any part of the Property or any Interest in the Property is sold or transferred (or if Borrower is not a natural person and a beneficial interest in Borrower is sold or transferred) without Lender's prior written consent, Lender may require immediate payment in full of all sums secured by this Security Instrument. However, this option shall not be exercised by Lender if such exercise is prohibited by federal law.

If Lender exercises this option, Lender shall give Borrower notice of acceleration. The notice shall provide a period of not less than 30 days from the date the notice is given in accordance with Section 15 within which Borrower must pay all sums secured by this Security Instrument. If Borrower fails to pay these sums prior to the expiration of this period, Lender may invoke any remedies permitted by this Security Instrument without further notice or demand on Borrower.

19. Borrower's Right to Reinstate After Acceleration. If Borrower meets certain conditions, Borrower shall have the right to have enforcement of this Security Instrument discontinued at any time prior to the earliest of: (a) five days before sale of the Property pursuant to any power of sale contained in this Security Instrument; (b) such other period as Applicable Law might specify for the termination of Borrower's right to reinstate; or (c) entry of a judgment enforcing this Security Instrument. Those conditions are that Borrower: (a) pays Lender all sums which then would be due under this Security Instrument and the Note as if no acceleration had occurred; (b) cures any default of any other covenants or agreements; (c) pays all expenses incurred in enforcing this Security Instrument, including, but not limited to, reasonable attorneys' fees, property inspection and valuation fees, and other fees incurred for the purpose of protecting Lender's interest in the Property and rights under this Security Instrument; and (d) takes such action as Lender may reasonably require to assure that Lender's interest in the Property and rights under this Security Instrument, and Borrower's obligation to pay the sums secured by this Security Instrument, shall continue unchanged. Lender may require that Borrower pay such reinstatement sums and expenses in one or more of the following forms, as selected by Lender: (a) cash; (b) money order; (c) certified check, bank check, treasurer's check or cashier's check, provided any such check is drawn upon an institution whose deposits are insured by a federal agency, instrumentality or entity; or (d) Electronic Funds Transfer. Upon reinstatement by Borrower, this Security Instrument and obligations secured hereby shall remain fully effective as if no acceleration had occurred. However, this right to reinstate shall not apply in the case of acceleration under Section 18.

20. Sale of Note; Change of Loan Servicer; Notice of Grievance. The Note or a partial interest in the Note (together with this Security Instrument) can be sold one or more times without prior notice to Borrower. A sale might result in a change in the entity (known as the "Loan Servicer") that collects Periodic Payments due under the Note and this Security Instrument and performs other mortgage loan servicing obligations under the Note, this Security Instrument, and Applicable Law. There also might be one or more changes of the Loan Servicer unrelated to a sale of the Note. If there is a change of the Loan Servicer, Borrower will be given written notice of the change which will state the name and address of the new Loan Servicer, the address to which payments should be made and any other information RESPA requires in connection with a notice of transfer of servicing. If the Note is sold and thereafter the Loan is serviced by a Loan Servicer other than the purchaser of the Note, the mortgage loan servicing obligations to Borrower will remain with the Loan Servicer or be transferred to a successor Loan Servicer and are not assumed by the Note purchaser unless otherwise provided by the Note purchaser.

Neither Borrower nor Lender may commence, join, or be joined to any judicial action (as either an individual litigant or the member of a class) that arises from the other party's actions pursuant to this Security Instrument or that alleges that the other party has breached any provision of, or any duty owed by reason of, this Security Instrument, until such Borrower or

Lender has notified the other party (with such notice given in compliance with the requirements of Section 15) of such alleged breach and afforded the other party hereto a reasonable period after the giving of such notice to take corrective action. If Applicable Law provides a time period which must elapse before certain action can be taken, that time period will be deemed to be reasonable for purposes of this paragraph. The notice of acceleration and opportunity to cure given to Borrower pursuant to Section 22 and the notice of acceleration given to Borrower pursuant to Section 18 shall be deemed to satisfy the notice and opportunity to take corrective action provisions of this Section 20.

21. Hazardous Substances. As used in this Section 21: (a) "Hazardous Substances" are those substances defined as toxic or hazardous substances, pollutants, or wastes by Environmental Law and the following substances: gasoline, kerosene, other flammable or toxic petroleum products, toxic pesticides and herbicides, volatile solvents, materials containing asbestos or formaldehyde, and radioactive materials; (b) "Environmental Law" means federal laws and laws of the jurisdiction where the Property is located that relate to health, safety or environmental protection; (c) "Environmental Cleanup" includes any response action, remedial action, or removal action, as defined in Environmental Law; and (d) an "Environmental Condition" means a condition that can cause, contribute to, or otherwise trigger an Environmental Cleanup.

Borrower shall not cause or permit the presence, use, disposal, storage, or release of any Hazardous Substances, or threaten to release any Hazardous Substances, on or in the Property. Borrower shall not do, nor allow anyone else to do, anything affecting the Property (a) that is in violation of any Environmental Law, (b) which creates an Environmental Condition, or (c) which, due to the presence, use, or release of a Hazardous Substance, creates a condition that adversely affects the value of the Property. The preceding two sentences shall not apply to the presence, use, or storage on the Property of small quantities of Hazardous Substances that are generally recognized to be appropriate to normal residential uses and to maintenance of the Property (including, but not limited to, hazardous substances in consumer products).

Borrower shall promptly give Lender written notice of (a) any investigation, claim, demand, lawsuit or other action by any governmental or regulatory agency or private party involving the Property and any Hazardous Substance or Environmental Law of which Borrower has actual knowledge, (b) any Environmental Condition, including but not limited to, any spilling, leaking, discharge, release or threat of release of any Hazardous Substance, and (c) any condition caused by the presence, use or release of a Hazardous Substance which adversely affects the value of the Property. If Borrower learns, or is notified by any governmental or regulatory authority, or any private party, that any removal or other remediation of any Hazardous Substance affecting the Property is necessary, Borrower shall promptly take all necessary remedial actions in accordance with Environmental Law. Nothing herein shall create any obligation on Lender for an Environmental Cleanup.

N NON-UNIFORM COVENANTS. Borrower and Lender further covenant and agree as follows:

22. Acceleration; Remedies. Lender shall give notice to Borrower prior to acceleration following Borrower's breach of any covenant or agreement in this Security

Instrument (but not prior to acceleration under Section 18 unless Applicable Law provides otherwise). The notice shall specify: (a) the default; (b) the action required to cure the default; (c) a date, not less than 30 days from the date the notice is given to Borrower, by which the default must be cured; and (d) that failure to cure the default on or before the date specified in the notice may result in acceleration of the sums secured by this Security Instrument, foreclosure by judicial proceeding and sale of the Property. The notice shall further inform Borrower of the right to reinstate after acceleration and the right to assert in the foreclosure proceeding the non-existence of a default or any other defense of Borrower to acceleration and foreclosure. If the default is not cured on or before the date specified in the notice, Lender at its option may require immediate payment in full of all sums secured by this Security Instrument without further demand and may foreclose this Security Instrument by judicial proceeding. Lender shall be entitled to collect all expenses incurred in pursuing the remedies provided in this Section 22, including, but not limited to, reasonable attorneys' fees and costs of title evidence.

23. Release. Upon payment of all sums secured by this Security Instrument, Lender shall release this Security Instrument. Borrower shall pay any recordation costs. Lender may charge Borrower a fee for releasing this Security Instrument, but only if the fee is paid to a third party for services rendered and the charging of the fee is permitted under Applicable Law.

24. Attorneys' Fees. As used in this Security Instrument and the Note, "attorneys' fees" shall include any attorneys' fees awarded by an appellate court and any attorneys' fees incurred in a bankruptcy proceeding.

25. Jury Trial Waiver. The Borrower hereby waives any right to a trial by jury in any action, proceeding, claim, or counterclaim, whether in contract or tort, at law or in equity, arising out of or in any way related to this Security Instrument or the Note.

BY SIGNING BELOW, Borrower accepts and agrees to the terms and covenants contained in this Security Instrument and in any rider(s) executed by Borrower and recorded with it.

Harry Homeowner
_____   _____
Borrower   Borrower

STATE OF FLORIDA
COUNTY OF **Pinellas**

    The foregoing instrument was acknowledged before me this **1st** *day of* **March** *,* **2001** *(year), by* **Harry Homeowner** *(name of person acknowledging)*

Nancy Notary *(Signature*   *(Seal)*
Nancy Notary

(Name of Notary printed, typed or stamped)
___ *Personally known OR*

x *Produced identification*
Type of identification produced: **Driver's License** _____

Option To Purchase Real Estate

THIS OPTION is made and entered into this __1st__ day of __October__ 20 __00__ by and between __Harry Homeowner__ hereinafter referred to as "Optionor," and __Ira Investor__ and/or assigns, hereinafter referred to as "Optionee".

WITNESSETH, that for and in consideration of $ __100.00__ and the mutual promises and covenants hereinafter set forth, the parties hereto agree as follows:

1. Option to Purchase Real Property. Optionor grants unto Optionee the exclusive right to purchase the real property described exhibit "A" annexed hereto.

2. Term of Option. This option shall commence on __Oct 1st__ 20 __00__ and expire on __October 1__, 20 __01__.

3. Terms of Sale. The terms of sale shall be: __Cash__

The following items shall be prorated at closing:
__property taxes, HOA dues, water/sewer, rents__

All personal property, appliances, attachments and fixtures shall be included in said sale except:

__Hot tub__

The Optionor shall convey title by a good and marketable __Warranty__ deed and shall furnish a policy of insurance from a reputable title insurance company.

4. Extension of Option Period. Upon payment of $ __500.00__, Optionee shall have the right to extend this option by __1__ years under the same terms and conditions.

5. Notice of Exercise. This option may be exercised at any time during the option period as described above, and Optionee may exercise said option with or without notice to Optionor.

6. Escrow of Closing Documents. All documents necessary for title transfer, including, but not limited to a warranty deed and bill of sale, shall be executed and held in escrow with an escrow agent of Optionee's choosing. Optionor shall execute a deed of trust or mortgage in favor of Optionee to secure performance of this agreement.

7. Insurance. Optionor shall protect Optionee's interest by maintaining hazard insurance upon the property, naming the Optionee as additional insured. In the event of destruction in whole or in part of the property, Optionee shall have the option to proceed with the closing and accept the insurance proceeds for said damage, or to declare this agreement null and void, releasing both parties from any obligations hereunder, except for the return of monies paid by Optionee which shall become immediately due and payable from the insurance proceeds.

8. Other Encumbrances. Optionor representing that the following liens and encumbrances currently exist on the property:
__1st mortgage to ABC Savings & Loan__

Optionor covenants that he will not further impair or encumber the property without Optionee's express written permission. In the event Optionor defaults on the payment of any of said security instruments, Optionee shall have the right to cure and/or satisfy said security instruments, and, in this event, shall be entitled to a 18% interest on actual expenses incurred in doing so.

9. Assignment: Optionee shall be permitted the right of assignment of this option.

10. <u>Agreement Binding</u>. This Agreement shall be binding upon the parties hereto and their respective heirs, administrators, successors, and assigns.

11.<u>Governing Law</u>. This agreement, and all transactions contemplated hereby, shall be governed by, construed and enforced in accordance with the laws of the State of __Colorado__.
In the event that litigation results from or arises out of this Agreement or the performance thereof, the parties agree to reimburse the prevailing party's reasonable attorney's fees, court costs, and all other expenses, whether or not taxable by the court as costs, in addition to any other relief to which the prevailing party may be entitled.

IN WITNESS WHEREOF, the parties hereto have hereunto set their hands and seals the day and year first above written.

Harry Homeowner
_____   _____
Optionor   Optionor

On __March 1__, 20 _01_, before me, **Nancy Notary**_____, a notary public in and for said state personally appeared __Harry Homeowner_____, personally known to me (or proved to me based upon satisfactory evidence) to be the person(s) whose name(s) are subscribed to the within instrument and acknowledged that (s)he/they executed the same in his/her/their signature on the instrument the person(s) or entity on behalf of which they acted, executed the instrument.

Nancy Notary
_____
Signature of Notary   NOTARY SEAL

My commission expires__*3/1/2003*_____

EXHIBIT "A" – Legal Description of Real Property

Lot 1, Block 2, Breezy Hills 3rd Filing, City & County of Denver, State of Colorado also known by street address as 123 Main Street, Denver, CO 80231

WRAP AROUND MORTGAGE RIDER

Rider and addendum to Security Instrument dated __May 12_____, 20_02____

The attached security instrument is a "wrap-around" mortgage/deed of trust subordinate to a certain mortgage/deed of trust dated _____Nov 1st_____, 20 _00____, executed in favor of First Capital Mortgage Group, Inc._____ and currently held by Countrywide Home Loans, Inc._____ in the original principal amount of $_129,000.00_____, which was recorded on the __15th____ day of __Dec_____, 20__00___ in the county records of ___Pleasant_____ County, State Anystate_____ as follows:

Book 6671, Pg 3242 Recording #2000374683

Borrower agrees to comply with all the terms and conditions of the above described mortgage, including, but not limited to, those concerning taxes and insurance, other than with respect to the payment of principal or interest due under said mortgage. If Borrower herein shall fail to comply with all the terms, provisions and conditions of said mortgage so as to result in a default thereunder (other than with respect to payments of principal or interest due), that failure on the part of Borrower herein shall constitute a default under this security instrument and shall entitle the lender, at its option, to exercise any and all rights and remedies given this security instrument in the event of a default under this security instrument.

If the lender hereunder shall default in making any required payment of principal or interest under the above described mortgage or deed of trust, the Borrower shall have the right to advance funds necessary to cure that default and all funds so advanced by Borrower shall be credited against the next installment of principal and interest due under the Note secured by this security instrument.

_Ira Investor_____   _____
Borrower   Borrower

State of __Anystate_____)
County of __Pleasant_____) ss:

On __May 12____, 20_02__, before me, _____Nancy Notary_____, a notary public in and for said state personally appeared _____Ira Investor_____ personally known to me (or proved to me based upon satisfactory evidence) to be the person(s) whose name(s) are subscribed to the within instrument and acknowledged that (s)he/they executed the same in his/her/their signature on the instrument the person(s) or entity on behalf of which they acted, executed the instrument.

_Nancy Notary_____ [NOTARY SEAL]
Signature of Notary
My commission expires _3/1/2003_

RECORDING REQUESTED BY

Author's Note:

This is an example of a "wraparound" deal discussed in Chapter Nine. Note that the interest rate on the balance of the sales price is actually LOWER than the interest rate on the underlying financing, yet the payment is essentially the same (since the outstanding balance due the seller is less than the balance due on his underlying loan).

This form of land contract is commonly used in California, containing a "power of sale" provision which allows the seller to foreclose the property in the same manner as a deed of trust. Form provided courtesy of First Tuesday, RIVERSIDE, CA (909) 781-7300

AND WHEN RECORDED MAIL TO

Name ⌈   ⌉
Street
Address
City &
State ⌊   ⌋

SPACE ABOVE THIS LINE FOR RECORDER'S USE

INSTALLMENT LAND CONTRACT
(All-Inclusive with Power of Sale)

Items left blank or unchecked are not applicable.

This Agreement, made this **1st** day of **July, 2002** ,between
Mark Motivated , called Vendor,
Ira Investor , called Vendee,
whose address is **PO BOX 12345, Los Angeles, CA 90001** ,
(number and street)   (city)   (state) (zip)
Regarding the real property in the City of **Pleasant** , County of **Los Angeles** California, described as:

Lot 26, Block 7, Pleasantville Subdivision 3rd Filing

1. Subject to the following trust deeds and notes referred to as Underlying Obligations:

    1.1 A trust deed recorded on **5/12/1998** , as Instrument No. **98-23948** in Official Records of **Los Angeles** County, California, executed by **Mark Motivated** as Trustor in which **ABC Savings & Loan** is Beneficiary, securing a note in the original amount of $ **150,000.00** with an unpaid balance of $ **$144,570.00** payable in installments of $ **$1,153.37** monthly including **8.5%** percent annual interest ☐ VIR, ☒ plus payments for impounds.

    1.2 A trust deed recorded on _____ , as Instrument No. _____ in Official Records of _____ County, California executed by _____ as Trustor in which _____ is Beneficiary, securing a note in the original amount of $_____ with an unpaid balance of $_____ payable in installments of $_____ monthly including _____ percent annual interest all due _____ .

    1.3 ☐ See attached addendum for additional Underlying Obligations.

    1.4 Vendor to remain responsible for and to pay all amounts called for in the Underlying Obligations.

2. **Vendee hereby purchases the property for the price of** . . . . $ **$175,000.00**

    2.1 The cash down payment on the price on entering into this agreement is the amount of. . . . $ **$10,000.00**

    2.2 The balance of the purchase price is the sum of . . . . $ **$165,000.00** , on unpaid principal bearing interest from date of ☒ agreement, OR ☐ _____ at the annual rate of **7.5** percent, payable in installments of **$1,153.70** DOLLARS, or more, on the **1st** day of each consecutive month beginning on the **1st** day of **August, 2002** , and continuing until **July 31st 2008** , when the principal is due and payable.

3. **Vendor retains legal title for the purpose of securing payment of:**

    a) the balance of the purchase price;

    b) any additional sums and interest hereafter loaned by Vendor to the Vendee, or their assignee, evidenced by a promissory note or notes, referencing this agreement as security for payment;

    c) the Vendor's charge for a statement regarding the secured obligations requested by or for Vendee; and

    d) the performance of each provision contained in this agreement.

Vendee agrees:

4. **Condition of Property** — To keep the property in good condition and repair; not to remove or demolish any building; to complete and restore any building which may be constructed, damaged or destroyed; to comply with all laws affecting the property or requiring any alterations or improvements to be made; not to commit or permit waste; to cultivate, irrigate, fertilize, fumigate, prune and do all other acts which from the character or use of the property may be reasonably necessary.

5. **Hazard Insurance** — Vendee will continuously maintain hazard insurance against loss by fire, hazards included within the term "extended coverage," and any other hazards for which the Vendor requires insurance. The insurance shall be maintained in the amounts and for the periods the Vendor

requires. The insurance carrier providing the insurance shall be chosen by Vendee, subject to Vendor's approval, which shall not be unreasonably withheld. All insurance policies shall be acceptable to Vendor, and contain loss payable clauses in form acceptable to Vendor. Vendor shall have the right to hold policies and renewals.

In the event of loss, Vendee shall promptly notify the insurance carrier and Vendor. Vendor may make proof of loss if not made promptly by Vendee. Vendor may place the proceeds in a non-interest bearing account to be used for the cost of reconstruction of the damaged improvements. If Vendee fails to reconstruct, Vendor may receive and apply the loan proceeds to the principal debt hereby secured, without a showing of impairment.

— — — — — — — — *PAGE ONE OF TWO — FORM 165* — — — — — — — — —

6. Indemnity — To appear in and defend any action or proceeding purporting to affect the security, or the rights and powers of Vendor; and to pay all costs and expenses.

7. Taxes & Senior Encumbrances — To pay: all taxes and assessments affecting the property, including water stock assessments at least ten days before delinquency; all encumbrances, charges and liens, with interest, on the property when due, which are not the responsibility of the Vendor and are or appear to be senior to this agreement; and all expenses of this agreement.

8. Acts & Advances to Protect the Security — If Vendee fails to make any payment or to perform any act provided for in this agreement, then Vendor may, at the option of the Vendor and without notice, and without releasing Vendee from any obligation under this agreement:

(a) make or do the same to the extent necessary to protect the security, Vendor being authorized to enter upon the property to do so;

(b) appear in or commence any action or proceeding purporting to affect the security, or the rights or powers of Vendor;

(c) pay, purchase, contest or settle any encumbrance, charge or lien that appears to be senior to this agreement.

In exercising the power of this provision, Vendor may incur necessary expenses and reasonable attorney fees.

Vendee to pay immediately all sums expended by Vendor provided for in this agreement, with interest from date of expenditure at the same rate as the principal debt hereby secured.

Vendor and Vendee agree:

9. Assignment of Damages — Vendee assigns to Vendor any award of damages made in connection with:

(a) condemnation for use of or injury to the property by the public, or conveyance in lieu of condemnation; or

(b) injury to the property by any third party.

10. Waiver — By accepting payment of any sum due after its due date, Vendor does not waive Vendor's right to either require prompt payment when due of all other sums or to declare default for failure to pay. Vendor may waive a default of any provision of this agreement, by consent or acquiescence, without waiving any prior or subsequent default.

11. Conveyance of Title — Vendor to convey title free of liens and encumbrances to Vendee upon Vendee's payment of all sums due to Vendor under this agreement.

11.1 On conveyance of title from Vendor to Vendee on full performance of this agreement by Vendee, the interest of Vendor and Vendee under this agreement will be insured by a title insurance policy obtained from **any reputable** Title Insurance Company, premium to be paid by [X] Vendor, OR ☐ Vendee.

11.2 On Vendee's deposit into escrow of all sums and instruments due to Vendor under this agreement and payment of all customary escrow costs and charges, Vendor to deposit into the escrow all instruments and instructions necessary to convey title and fully perform this agreement.

12. Due-on-sale — Should Vendee sell, transfer or convey any interest in the property, legal or equitable, either voluntarily or by operation of law, Vendor may, at Vendor's option, declare all sums secured by this agreement immediately due and payable.

13. Assignment of Rents — Vendee hereby assigns and transfers to Vendor all the rights, title and interest in rents generated by the property, including rents now due, past due or to become due under any use of the property, to be applied to the obligations secured by this agreement.

Prior to a default on the trust deed by the Vendee, Vendee shall collect and retain the rents. On default by Vendee, and without the necessity of the Vendor to make demand or take possession of the property in person, by agent or by court appointed receiver, Vendor shall immediately be entitled to possession of all unpaid rents.

14. Acceleration — If payment of any indebtedness or performance of this agreement is in default, then Vendor may at Vendor's option, without notice, declare all sums secured immediately due and payable by:

(a) commencing suit for their recovery by foreclosure of this lien; or

(b) delivering to Trustee a written notice declaring default with demand for sale; a written notice of default and election to sell to be recorded.

15. Power of Sale — On default under any obligation of this agreement and acceleration of all sums due, Vendor may elect to proceed with a power of sale by a trustee substituted under Civil Code §2934a, noticed and held in accordance with California Civil Code §2924 et seq.

15.1 The undersigned Vendee requests a copy of any Notice of Default and of any Notice of Sale hereunder be mailed to Vendee at the address herein set forth.

16. Prepayment Penalty — Any principal paid in addition to regular installments will, if so requested by Vendee, be paid by Vendor to holders of Underlying Obligations for a reduction in the principal. If the holders are entitled to a prepayment penalty Vendee shall pay the amount to Vendor for payment of the penalty. The prepayment penalty will not reduce the unpaid balance of principal or accrued interest on the debt remaining on this agreement.

17. Cure of Default — If Vendor defaults in his performance on this agreement, including payment of the Underlying Obligations, Vendee may cure the default and credit the payments against the principal and interest due under this agreement, or recover from Vendor, on demand, the amount of the payments including interest thereon at the note rate.

18. Successors, Assigns & Pledgees — This agreement is for the benefit of, and binds all parties, their heirs, legatees, devisees, administrators, executors, successors and assigns. The term Vendor shall mean the holder and owner of the agreement, or, if the agreement has been pledged, the pledgee.

19. Vendee's Offset Statement — Within ten days of Vendee's receipt of a written request by Vendor, Vendee shall execute a written estoppel affidavit identifying for the benefit of any assignee or successor in interest of the Vendor: the then owner of the secured property; the terms of the secured debt, including its remaining principal balance; any taxes or assessments due on the secured property; that the secured debt is valid and the Vendee received full and valid consideration for it; and that the Vendee understands the debt and this agreement are being assigned.

20. Final Balloon Payment Notice — This note is subject to Section 2966 of the Civil Code, which provides that the holder of this note shall give written notice to the Vendee, or his successor in interest, of prescribed information at least 90 and not more than 150 days before any balloon payment is due.

21. Addenda — The following checked addenda are a part of this agreement: ☐ Impounds rider for taxes & insurance; ☐ Owner-occupancy rider; ☐ Contract collection rider; ☐ _____.

22. Attorneys Fees — The prevailing party in any dispute shall be entitled to attorneys fees and costs.

STATE OF CALIFORNIA }
COUNTY OF Los Angeles }
On this 1st day of July, 2002
before me, Nancy Notary ,
(name of notary public)
personally appeared Mark Motivated & Ira Investor ,
(name of principal)

personally known to me (or proved to me on the basis of satisfactory evidence) to be the person(s) whose name(s) is/are subscribed to the within instrument and acknowledged to me that or he/she/they executed the same in his/her/their authorized capacity(ies), and that by his/her/their signature(s) on the instrument the person(s), or the entity upon behalf of which the person(s) acted, executed the instrument.

WITNESS my hand and official seal.

Signature *Nancy Notary*
(Signature of notary public)

Date: 7/1/2002

Vendor: *Mark Motivated*

Vendor: _____

Date: 7/1/2002

Vendee: *Ira Investor*

Vendee: _____

FORM 165   09-96   ©1996 first tuesday, P.O. BOX 20069, RIVERSIDE, CA 92516 (909) 781-7300

RECORDING REQUESTED BY

XYZ ESCROW COMPANY

AND WHEN RECORDED MAIL TO

XYZ ESCROW, PO BOX 12, San Diego, CA 92123

SUBORDINATION AGREEMENT

THIS SUBORDINATION AGREEMENT, made this <u>12th</u> day of <u>April</u>, 20 <u>02</u>, by and between <u>Harry Homeowner</u>

owner of real property described herein ("Owner,") and <u>ABC Home Loan Corporation</u>

_____, the current holder of the security interest hereinafter described herein ("Beneficiary");

    WHEREAS, OWNER has executed a security instrument, dated <u>Jan 15th</u>, 20 <u>02</u>, to <u>XYZ ESCROW COMPANY</u>, as trustee,

to secure a note in the sum of $ <u>150,000.00</u>, dated <u>Jan 15th</u> 20 <u>02</u>, in favor of <u>ABC Home Loan Corporation</u> as beneficiary the real property as described in the annexed exhibit "A" hereto,

which instrument was recorded on <u>Jan 21st</u>, 20 <u>02</u>, in the county of <u>San Diego</u>

under the following recording information <u>Recording #34567-2002, Book 3456, Page 454</u>; and

    WHEREAS, Owner has executed, or is about to execute, a deed of trust and note in the sum of $ <u>100,000.00</u>

dated <u>April 12th, 2002</u>, in favor of <u>US Savings Bank</u>

("Lender"), payable with interest and upon the terms and conditions described therein, which deed of trust is to be recorded concurrently herewith; and

    WHEREAS, it is a condition precedent to obtaining said loan that said deed of trust last above mentioned shall unconditionally be and remain at all times a lien or charge upon the land hereinbefore described, prior and superior to the lien or charge of the security instrument first above mentioned; and

    WHEREAS, Lender is willing to make said loan provided the deed of trust securing the same is a lien or charge upon the above described property prior and superior to the lien or charge of the security instrument first above mentioned and provided that Beneficiary will specifically and unconditionally subordinate the lien or charge of the security instrument first above mentioned to the lien or charge of the deed of trust in favor of Lender; and

    WHEREAS, it is to the mutual benefit of the parties hereto that Lender make such loan to Owner; and Beneficiary is willing that the deed of trust securing the same shall, when recorded, constitute a lien or charge upon said land which is unconditionally prior and superior to the lien or charge of the deed of trust first above mentioned.

    NOW, THEREFORE, in consideration of the mutual benefits accruing to the parties hereto and other valuable consideration, the receipt and sufficiency of which consideration is hereby acknowledged, and in order to induce Lender to make the loan above referred to, it is hereby declared, understood and agreed as follows:

(1) That said deed of trust securing said note in favor of Lender, and any renewals or extensions thereof, shall unconditionally be and remain at all times a lien or charge on the property therein described, prior and superior to the lien or charge of the security instrument first above mentioned.

(2) That Lender would not make its loan above described without this subordination agreement.

(3) That this agreement shall be the whole and only agreement between the parties hereto with regard to the subordination of the lien or charge of the security instrument first above mentioned to the lien or charge of the deed of trust in favor of Lender above referred to and shall supersede and cancel any prior agreements as to such, or any, subordination including, but not limited to, those provisions, if any, contained in the deed of trust first above mentioned, which provide for the subordination of the lien or charge thereof to a deed or deeds of trust or to a mortgage or mortgages to be thereafter executed.

Beneficiary declares, agrees and acknowledges that

(a) He consents to and approves (i) all provisions of the note and deed of trust in favor of Lender above referred to, and (ii) all agreements, including but not limited to any loan or escrow agreements, between Owner and Lender for the disbursement of the proceeds of Lender's loan;

(b) Lender in making disbursements pursuant to any such agreement is under no obligation or duty to, nor has Lender represented that it will, see to the application of such proceeds by the person or persons to whom Lender disburses such proceeds and any application or use of such proceeds for purposes other than those provided for in such agreement or agreements shall not defeat the subordination herein made in whole or in party;

(c) He intentionally and unconditionally waives, relinquishes and subordinates the lien or charge of the security instrument first above mentioned in favor of the lien or charge upon said land of the deed of trust in favor of Lender above referred to and understands that in reliance upon, and in consideration of, this waiver, relinquishment and subordination specific loans and advances are being and will be made and, as part and parcel thereof, specific monetary and other obligations are being and will be entered into which would not be made or entered into but for said reliance upon this waiver, relinquishment and subordination; and

_John Smith, Vice Pres_____   _Harry Homeowner_____
Beneficiary   Owner

STATE OF CALIFORNIA
COUNTY OF _San Diego_____} SS.

On _April 12th, 2002_____ before me, _Nancy Notary_____,
personally appeared _John Smith, Vice President of ABC Home Loan Corporation and Harry Homeowner_____
personally known to me (or proved to me on the basis of satisfactory evidence) to be the person(s) whose name(s) is/are subscribed to the within instrument and acknowledged to me that he/she/they executed the same in his/her/their authorized capacity(ies), and that by his/her/their signature(s) on the instrument the person(s), or the entity upon behalf of which the person(s) acted, executed the instrument.

WITNESS my hand and official seal.

Notary Signature_Nancy Notary_____

EXHIBIT "A": REAL PROPERTY DESCRIPTION:

LOTS 12, 13 of BLOCK 35, SUNNY DAZE SUBDIVISION,
THIRD FILING, COUNTY OF SAN DIEGO, STATE OF CALIFORNIA

KNOWN BY STREET ADDRESS AS:
12345 Happy Canyon Road, San Diego, CA 93746

APPENDIX D

Appraisal of Real Property

APPRAISAL OF REAL PROPERTY

LOCATED AT:
12506 E Cornell Ave

FOR:

AS OF:
12/02/2006

BY:

Residential Appraiser

SUMMARY OF SALIENT FEATURES

SUBJECT INFORMATION	Subject Address	12506 E Cornell Ave
	Legal Description	Unit 103 Bldg 15 As Per Condo Declaration Recorded In B3164 P592 Spinnaker Run (
	City	
	County	
	State	CO
	Zip Code	
	Census Tract	0070.22
	Map Reference	317
SALES PRICE	Sale Price	$
	Date of Sale	
CLIENT	Borrower / Client	
	Lender	
DESCRIPTION OF IMPROVEMENTS	Size (Square Feet)	1,022
	Price per Square Foot	$
	Location	Spinnaker Run
	Age	26 Yrs
	Condition	Above Average
	Total Rooms	5
	Bedrooms	2
	Baths	2
APPRAISER	Appraiser	
	Date of Appraised Value	12/02/2006
VALUE	Final Estimate of Value	$ 107,000

Platinum Appraisal Group (303) 437-0189

Individual Condominium Unit Appraisal Report　　File # 6153

The purpose of this summary appraisal report is to provide the lender/client with an accurate, and adequately supported, opinion of the market value of the subject property.

SUBJECT

Property Address 12506 E Cornell Ave	Unit # 103　　City	State CO　Zip Code
Borrower	Owner of Public Record	County Arapahoe

Legal Description　Unit 103 Bldg 15 As Per Condo Declaration Recorded In B3164 P592 Spinnaker Run Condos

Assessor's Parcel # 1973-362-221-23	Tax Year 2005	R.E. Taxes $ 652.75
Project Name Spinnaker Run Condos	Phase # Unknown　Map Reference 317	Census Tract 0070.22
Occupant ☐ Owner ☒ Tenant ☐ Vacant	Special Assessments $ 0.00	HOA $ 150.00 ☐ per year ☒ per month

Property Rights Appraised ☒ Fee Simple ☐ Leasehold ☐ Other (describe)

Assignment Type ☐ Purchase Transaction ☒ Refinance Transaction ☐ Other (describe)

Lender/Client　　　　　　　　　　Address

Is the subject property currently offered for sale or has it been offered for sale in the twelve months prior to the effective date of this appraisal?　☐ Yes ☒ No

Report data source(s) used, offering price(s), and date(s).

CONTRACT

I ☐ did ☐ did not analyze the contract for sale for the subject purchase transaction. Explain the results of the analysis of the contract for sale or why the analysis was not performed.

Contract Price $　　Date of Contract　　Is the property seller the owner of public record? ☐ Yes ☐ No Data Source(s)

Is there any financial assistance (loan charges, sale concessions, gift or downpayment assistance, etc.) to be paid by any party on behalf of the borrower?　☐ YES ☐ NO

If Yes, report the total dollar amount and describe the items to be paid.

NEIGHBORHOOD

Note: Race and the racial composition of the neighborhood are not appraisal factors.

Neighborhood Characteristics			Condominium Unit Housing Trends			Condominium Housing			Present Land Use %	
Location ☐ Urban ☒ Suburban ☐ Rural			Property Values ☐ Increasing ☒ Stable ☐ Declining			PRICE	AGE		One-Unit	85 %
Built-Up ☐ Over 75% ☒ 25-75% ☐ Under 25%			Demand/Supply ☐ Shortage ☒ In Balance ☐ Over Supply			$ (000)	(yrs)		2-4 Unit	5 %
Growth ☐ Rapid ☒ Stable ☐ Slow			Marketing Time ☒ Under 3 mths ☐ 3-6 mths ☐ Over 6 mths			59	Low	5	Multi-Family	%
Neighborhood Boundaries　Bounded on the north by Mississippi Avenue, on the east by I 225, on the						250	High	50	Commercial	10 %
south by Parker Road, and on the west by Peoria Street.						100	Pred.	25	Other	%

Neighborhood Description　The subject property is located in an area of average to good quality single family and multi family condominiums similar in size and design to the subject. No adverse conditions were evident. Proximity to employment, recreation, and all other services is acceptable. The subject appears to be maintained in an acceptable manner and consistent with the neighborhood. This appraisal is subject to all easements

Market Conditions (including support for the above conclusions)　Market conditions in the subject area are acceptable. Moderate supply and demand and low interest rates are having a stabalizing affect on values in the subject area. Typical marketing time in the subject area is less than three months.

PROJECT SITE

Topography Generally Level	Size Typical for area	Density Average	View Neighborhood

Specific Zoning Classification Residential　　Zoning Description Residential - Condominium

Zoning Compliance ☒ Legal ☐ Legal Nonconforming – Do the zoning regulations permit rebuilding to current density? ☐ Yes ☐ No

☐ No Zoning ☐ Illegal (describe)

Is the highest and best use of subject property as improved (or as proposed per plans and specifications) the present use? ☒ Yes ☐ No If No, describe

Utilities　Public　Other (describe)		Public　Other (describe)	Off-site Improvements – Type	Public	Private
Electricity ☒ ☐		Water ☒ ☐	Street Asphalt	☒	☐
Gas ☒ ☐		Sanitary Sewer ☒ ☐	Alley None	☐	☐

FEMA Special Flood Hazard Area ☐ Yes ☒ No　FEMA Flood Zone X　FEMA Map # 08005C0190J　FEMA Map Date 8/16/1995

Are the utilities and off-site improvements typical for the market area? ☒ Yes ☐ No If No, describe

Are there any adverse site conditions or external factors (easements, encroachments, environmental conditions, land uses, etc.)? ☐ Yes ☒ No If Yes, describe

PROJECT INFORMATION

Data source(s) for project information　PDC/County Records

Project Description ☐ Detached ☒ Row or Townhouse ☐ Garden ☐ Mid-Rise ☐ High-Rise ☐ Other (describe)

General Description	General Description	Subject Phase		If Project Completed		If Project Incomplete	
# of Stories Three	Exterior Walls Frm/Sid	# of Units	291	# of Phases	Unkn	# of Planned Phases	
# of Elevators 0	Roof Surface Comp	# of Units Completed	291	# of Units	291	# of Planned Units	
☒ Existing ☐ Proposed	Total # Parking 326	# of Units For Sale	12	# of Units for Sale	12	# of Units for Sale	
☐ Under Construction	Ratio (spaces/units) 1:12	# of Units Sold	291	# of Units Sold	291	# of Units Sold	
Year Built 1980	Type Open	# of Units Rented	106	# of Units Rented	106	# of Units Rented	
Effective Age 7-9	Guest Parking 15	# of Owner Occupied Units	185	# of Owner Occupied Units	185	# of Owner Occupied Units	

Project Primary Occupancy ☒ Principle Residence ☐ Second Home or Recreational ☐ Tenant

Is the developer/builder in control of the Homeowners' Association (HOA)? ☐ Yes ☒ No

Management Group - ☒ Homeowners' Association ☐ Developer ☐ Management Agent - Provide name of management company.

Does any single entity (the same individual, investor group, corporation, etc.) own more than 10% of the total units in the project? ☐ Yes ☒ No If Yes, Describe

Was the project created by the conversion of existing building(s) into a condominium? ☐ Yes ☒ No If Yes, describe the original use and date of conversion.

Are the units, common elements, and recreation facilities complete (including any planned rehabilitation for a condominium conversion)? ☒ Yes ☐ No If No, describe

Is there any commercial space in the project? ☐ Yes ☒ No If Yes, describe and indicate the overall percentage of the commercial space.

Freddie Mac Form 465 March 2005	Page 1 of 6	Fannie Mae Form 1073 March 2005

Individual Condominium Unit Appraisal Report   File # 6153

<table>
<tr><td colspan="2">Describe the condition of the project and quality of construction.   The subject is well maintained. Typical building has   floors with   units. Standard low rise style multi residential buildings.</td></tr>
<tr><td colspan="2">Describe the common elements and recreational facilities.</td></tr>
<tr><td colspan="2">Are any common elements leased to or by the Homeowners' Association? ☐ Yes ☒ No If Yes, describe the rental terms and options.</td></tr>
<tr><td colspan="2">Is the project subject to a ground rent? ☐ Yes ☒ No If Yes, $ per year (describe terms and conditions)</td></tr>
<tr><td colspan="2">Are the parking facilities adequate for the project size and type? ☒ Yes ☐ No If No, describe and comment on the effect on value and marketability.</td></tr>
<tr><td colspan="2">I ☐ did ☒ did not analyze the condominium project budget for the current year. Explain the results of the analysis of the budget (adequacy of fees, reserves, etc.), or why the analysis was not performed.   Was not made available to appraiser.</td></tr>
<tr><td colspan="2">Are there any other fees (other than regular HOA charges) for the use of the project facilities? ☐ Yes ☒ No   If Yes, report the charges and describe.</td></tr>
<tr><td colspan="2">Compared to other competitive projects of similar quality and design, the subject unit charge appears ☐ High ☒ Average ☐ Low If High or Low, describe</td></tr>
<tr><td colspan="2">Are there any special or unusual characteristics of the project (based on the condominium documents, HOA meetings, or other information) known to the appraiser? ☐ Yes ☒ No If Yes, describe and explain the effect on value and marketability.</td></tr>
</table>

PROJECT INFORMATION

PROJECT ANALYSIS

Unit Charge $ 150.00   per month X 12 = $ 1,800.00   per year   Annual assessment charge per year per square feet of gross living area = $ 1.76
Utilities included in the unit monthly assessment ☐ None ☐ Heat ☐ Air Conditioning ☐ Electricity ☐ Gas ☒ Water ☐ Sewer ☐ Cable ☐ Other (describe)

General Description	Interior	materials/condition	Amenities	Appliances	Car Storage
Floor # Ground	Floors	Carpet/Vinyl/Abv Avg	☒ Fireplace(s) # 1	☐ Refrigerator	☒ None
# of Levels One	Walls	Drywall/Abv Avg	☐ WoodStove(s) #	☒ Range/Oven	☐ Garage ☐ Covered ☐ Open
Heating Type FWA Fuel Gas	Trim/Finish	Wood/Paint/Abv Avg	☒ Deck/Patio Patio	☒ Disp ☐ Microwave	# of Cars
☒ Central AC ☐ Individual AC	Bath Wainscot	Tile/Above Average	☐ Porch/Balcony	☒ Dishwasher	☐ Assigned ☐ Owned
☐ Other (describe)	Doors	Hollow/Average	☐ Other	☐ Washer/Dryer	Parking Space #
Finished area **above** grade contains:	5 Rooms	2 Bedrooms	2 Bath(s)	1,022 Square Feet of Gross Living Area Above Grade	

Are the heating and cooling for the individual units separately metered? ☒ Yes ☐ No If No, describe and comment on compatibility to other projects in the market area.

Additional features (special energy efficient items, etc.)   Aluminum dual glaze windows and insulation.

Describe the condition of the property (including needed repairs, deterioration, renovations, remodeling, etc.).   The subject is in above average condition with no repairs indicated.

Are there any physical deficiencies or adverse conditions that affect the livability, soundness, or structural integrity of the property? ☐ Yes ☒ No If Yes, describe

Does the property generally conform to the neighborhood (functional utility, style, condition, use, construction, etc.)? ☒ Yes ☐ No If No, describe

UNIT DESCRIPTION

I ☒ did ☐ did not research the sale or transfer history of the subject property and comparable sales. If not, explain   No prior sales since last purchase.

My research ☐ did ☒ did not reveal any prior sales or transfers of the subject property for the three years prior to the effective date of this appraisal.
Data source(s)   MLS/County Records
My research ☐ did ☒ did not reveal any prior sales or transfers of the comparable sales for the year prior to the date of sale of the comparable sale.
Data source(s)   MLS/County Records
Report the results of the research and analysis of the prior sale or transfer history of the subject property and comparable sales (report additional prior sales on page 3).

ITEM	SUBJECT	COMPARABLE SALE #1	COMPARABLE SALE #2	COMPARABLE SALE #3
Date of Prior Sale/Transfer	05/14/2001	No prior sales for the	No prior sales for the	No prior sales for the
Price of Prior Sale/Transfer	115,000	past 12 months	past 12 months	past 12 months
Data Source(s)	MLS/County Records	MLS/County Records	MLS/County Records	MLS/County Records
Effective Date of Data Source(s)	1/01/2006	1/01/2006	1/01/2006	1/01/2006

Analysis of prior sale or transfer history of the subject property and comparable sales.   No prior sales since last purchase.

PRIOR SALE HISTORY

File No. 6153 Page #5

Individual Condominium Unit Appraisal Report   File # 6153

There are **12** comparable properties currently offered for sale in the subject neighborhood ranging in price from $ **59,500** to $ **91,900**.

There are **20** comparable sales in the subject neighborhood within the past twelve months ranging in sale price from $ **52,000** to $ **110,000**.

FEATURE	SUBJECT	COMPARABLE SALE # 1	+(-) $ Adjustment	COMPARABLE SALE # 2	+(-) $ Adjustment	COMPARABLE SALE # 3	+(-) $ Adjustment
Address and Unit #	12506 E Cornell Ave, # 103	3012 S. Ursula Circle #302 Aurora DOM 90		3063 S. Ursula Circle #102 Aurora DOM 96		12502 E. Evans Circle #C Aurora DOM 22	
Project Name and Phase	Spinnaker Run Condos Unknown	Spinnaker Run II Condos Unknown		Spinnaker Run Condos Unknown		Champagne At Willowridge Unknown	
Proximity to Subject		0.20 miles		0.26 miles		0.98 miles	
Sale Price	$	$ 109,000		$ 110,000		$ 109,900	
Sale Price/Gross Liv. Area	$ sq. ft.	$ 107.28 sq. ft.		$ 108.27 sq. ft.		$ 131.15 sq. ft.	
Data Source(s)		MLS/Broker		MLS/Broker		MLS/Broker	
Verification Source(s)		County Records		County Records		County Records	
VALUE ADJUSTMENTS	DESCRIPTION	DESCRIPTION	+(-) $ Adjustment	DESCRIPTION	+(-) $ Adjustment	DESCRIPTION	+(-) $ Adjustment
Sales or Financing Concessions		Conventional Concessions	-3,000	Conventional None		Conv No Pts Concessions	-3,000
Date of Sale/Time		01/27/2006		07/24/2006		02/28/2006	
Location	Spinnaker Run	Spinnaker Run		Spinnaker Run		Champagne	
Leasehold/Fee Simple	Fee Simple	Fee simple		Fee simple		Fee simple	
HOA Mo. Assessment	150.00	156.00		150.00		130.00	
Common Elements and Rec. Facilities	ExtMaint,HzdIns Wtr/Swr,Trash	ExtMaint,HzdIns Wtr/Swr,Trash		ExtMaint,HzdIns Wtr/Swr,Trash		ExtMaint,HzdIns Wtr/Swr,Trash	
Floor Location	Ground	Third		Ground		Ground	
View	Neighborhood	Neighborhood		Neighborhood		Neighborhood	
Design (Style)	Ranch	Ranch		Ranch		Ranch	
Quality of Construction	Average	Average		Average		Average	
Actual Age	26 Yrs	25 Yrs		25 Yrs		24 Yrs	
Condition	Above Average	Above Average		Above Average		Above Average	
Above Grade	Total 5 Bdrms. 2 Baths 2	Total 5 Bdrms. 2 Baths 2		Total 5 Bdrms. 2 Baths 2		Total 4 Bdrms. 1 Baths 1	+3,000
Room Count							
Gross Living Area	1,022 sq. ft.	1,016 sq. ft.		1,016 sq. ft.		838 sq. ft.	+4,600
Basement & Finished Rooms Below Grade	None N/A	None N/A		None N/A		None N/A	
Functional Utility	Average	Average		Average		Average	
Heating/Cooling	GFWA, A/C	GFWA, A/C		GFWA, A/C		GFWA, A/C	
Energy Efficient Items	Insul/Dual Glaze	Insul/Dual Glaze		Insul/Dual Glaze		Insul/Dual Glaze	
Garage/Carport	None	1 Car Att	-2,500	1 Car Det	-2,500	1 Car Att	-2,500
Porch/Patio/Deck	Patio	Balcony		Patio		Patio	
Fireplace	1 FP	1 FP		1 FP		1 FP	
Other	None	None		None		None	
Net Adjustment (Total)		☐ + ☒ - $	5,500	☐ + ☒ - $	2,500	☒ + ☐ - $	2,100
Adjusted Sale Price of Comparables		$ 103,500		$ 107,500		$ 112,000	

Summary of Sales Comparison Approach   See attached addendum for market data information.

Indicated Value by Sales Comparison Approach $ **107,000**

INCOME APPROACH TO VALUE (not required by Fannie Mae)

Estimated Monthly Market Rent $ _____ X Gross Rent Multiplier _____ = $ _____   Indicated Value by Income Approach _____

Summary of Income Approach (including support for market rent and GRM)

Indicated Value by: Sales Comparison Approach $ **107,000**   Income Approach (if developed) $ _____

Cost and Income approaches were not alternative methods to value. The direct sales comparison approach was given greatest weight as measures interaction of buyer and seller.

This appraisal is made ☒ "as is", ☐ subject to completion per plans and specifications on the basis of a hypothetical condition that the improvements have been completed, ☐ subject to the following repairs or alterations on the basis of a hypothetical condition that the repairs or alterations have been completed, or ☐ subject to the following required inspection based on the extraordinary assumption that the condition or deficiency does not require alteration or repair: NO CONDITIONS. The subject has been appraised in AS IS condition with no repairs indicated. All sales were confirmed by agent/broker and county records.

Based on a complete visual inspection of the interior and exterior areas of the subject property, defined scope of work, statement of assumptions and limiting conditions, and appraiser's certification, my (our) opinion of the market value, as defined, of the real property that is the subject of this report is $ **107,000** , as of **12/02/2006** , which is the date of inspection and the effective date of this appraisal.

Individual Condominium Unit Appraisal Report   File # 6153

This report form is designed to report an appraisal of a unit in a condominium project or a condominium unit in a planned unit development (PUD). This report form is not designed to report an appraisal of a manufactured home or a unit in a cooperative project.

This appraisal report is subject to the following scope of work, intended use, intended user, definition of market value, statement of assumptions and limiting conditions, and certifications. Modifications, additions, or deletions to the intended use, intended user, definition of market value, or assumptions and limiting conditions are not permitted. The appraiser may expand the scope of work to include any additional research or analysis necessary based on the complexity of this appraisal assignment. Modifications or deletions to the certifications are also not permitted. However, additional certifications that do not constitute material alterations to this appraisal report, such as those required by law or those related to the appraiser's continuing education or membership in an appraisal organization, are permitted.

SCOPE OF WORK: The scope of work for this appraisal is defined by the complexity of this appraisal assignment and the reporting requirements of this appraisal report form, including the following definition of market value, statement of assumptions and limiting conditions, and certifications. The appraiser must, at a minimum: (1) perform a complete visual inspection of the interior and exterior areas of the subject unit, (2) inspect and analyze the condominium project, (3) inspect the neighborhood, (4) inspect each of the comparable sales from at least the street, (5) research, verify, and analyze data from reliable public and/or private sources, and (6) report his or her analysis, opinions, and conclusions in this appraisal report.

INTENDED USE: The intended use of this appraisal report is for the lender/client to evaluate the property that is the subject of this appraisal for a mortgage finance transaction.

INTENDED USER: The intended user of this appraisal report is the lender/client.

MARKET VALUE: The most probable price which a property should bring in a competitive and open market under all conditions requisite to a fair sale, the buyer and seller, each acting prudently, knowledgeably and assuming the price is not affected by undue stimulus. Implicit in this definition is the consummation of a sale as of a specified date and the passing of title from seller to buyer under conditions whereby: (1) buyer and seller are typically motivated; (2) both parties are well informed or well advised, and each acting in what he or she considers his or her own best interest; (3) a reasonable time is allowed for exposure in the open market; (4) payment is made in terms of cash in U. S. dollars or in terms of financial arrangements comparable thereto; and (5) the price represents the normal consideration for the property sold unaffected by special or creative financing or sales concessions* granted by anyone associated with the sale.

*Adjustments to the comparables must be made for special or creative financing or sales concessions. No adjustments are necessary for those costs which are normally paid by sellers as a result of tradition or law in a market area; these costs are readily identifiable since the seller pays these costs in virtually all sales transactions. Special or creative financing adjustments can be made to the comparable property by comparisons to financing terms offered by a third party institutional lender that is not already involved in the property or transaction. Any adjustment should not be calculated on a mechanical dollar for dollar cost of the financing or concession but the dollar amount of any adjustment should approximate the market's reaction to the financing or concessions based on the appraiser's judgment.

STATEMENT OF ASSUMPTIONS AND LIMITING CONDITIONS: The appraiser's certification in this report is subject to the following assumptions and limiting conditions:

1. The appraiser will not be responsible for matters of a legal nature that affect either the property being appraised or the title to it, except for information that he or she became aware of during the research involved in performing this appraisal. The appraiser assumes that the title is good and marketable and will not render any opinions about the title.

2. The appraiser has provided a sketch in this appraisal report to show the approximate dimensions of the improvements. The sketch is included only to assist the reader in visualizing the property and understanding the appraiser's determination of its size.

3. The appraiser has examined the available flood maps that are provided by the Federal Emergency Management Agency (or other data sources) and has noted in this appraisal report whether any portion of the subject site is located in an identified Special Flood Hazard Area. Because the appraiser is not a surveyor, he or she makes no guarantees, express or implied, regarding this determination.

4. The appraiser will not give testimony or appear in court because he or she made an appraisal of the property in question, unless specific arrangements to do so have been made beforehand, or as otherwise required by law.

5. The appraiser has noted in this appraisal report any adverse conditions (such as needed repairs, deterioration, the presence of hazardous wastes, toxic substances, etc.) observed during the inspection of the subject property or that he or she became aware of during the research involved in performing this appraisal. Unless otherwise stated in this appraisal report, the appraiser has no knowledge of any hidden or unapparent physical deficiencies or adverse conditions of the property (such as, but not limited to, needed repairs, deterioration, the presence of hazardous wastes, toxic substances, adverse environmental conditions, etc.) that would make the property less valuable, and has assumed that there are no such conditions and makes no guarantees or warranties, express or implied. The appraiser will not be responsible for any such conditions that do exist or for any engineering or testing that might be required to discover whether such conditions exist. Because the appraiser is not an expert in the field of environmental hazards, this appraisal report must not be considered as an environmental assessment of the property.

6. The appraiser has based his or her appraisal report and valuation conclusion for an appraisal that is subject to satisfactory completion, repairs, or alterations on the assumption that the completion, repairs, or alterations of the subject property will be performed in a professional manner.

Individual Condominium Unit Appraisal Report
File # 6153

APPRAISER'S CERTIFICATION: The Appraiser certifies and agrees that:

1. I have, at a minimum, developed and reported this appraisal in accordance with the scope of work requirements stated in this appraisal report.

2. I performed a complete visual inspection of the interior and exterior areas of the subject property. I reported the condition of the improvements in factual, specific terms. I identified and reported the physical deficiencies that could affect the livability, soundness, or structural integrity of the property.

3. I performed this appraisal in accordance with the requirements of the Uniform Standards of Professional Appraisal Practice that were adopted and promulgated by the Appraisal Standards Board of The Appraisal Foundation and that were in place at the time this appraisal report was prepared.

4. I developed my opinion of the market value of the real property that is the subject of this report based on the sales comparison approach to value. I have adequate comparable market data to develop a reliable sales comparison approach for this appraisal assignment. I further certify that I considered the cost and income approaches to value but did not develop them, unless otherwise indicated in this report.

5. I researched, verified, analyzed, and reported on any current agreement for sale for the subject property, any offering for sale of the subject property in the twelve months prior to the effective date of this appraisal, and the prior sales of the subject property for a minimum of three years prior to the effective date of this appraisal, unless otherwise indicated in this report.

6. I researched, verified, analyzed, and reported on the prior sales of the comparable sales for a minimum of one year prior to the date of sale of the comparable sale, unless otherwise indicated in this report.

7. I selected and used comparable sales that are locationally, physically, and functionally the most similar to the subject property.

8. I have not used comparable sales that were the result of combining a land sale with the contract purchase price of a home that has been built or will be built on the land.

9. I have reported adjustments to the comparable sales that reflect the market's reaction to the differences between the subject property and the comparable sales.

10. I verified, from a disinterested source, all information in this report that was provided by parties who have a financial interest in the sale or financing of the subject property.

11. I have knowledge and experience in appraising this type of property in this market area.

12. I am aware of, and have access to, the necessary and appropriate public and private data sources, such as multiple listing services, tax assessment records, public land records and other such data sources for the area in which the property is located.

13. I obtained the information, estimates, and opinions furnished by other parties and expressed in this appraisal report from reliable sources that I believe to be true and correct.

14. I have taken into consideration the factors that have an impact on value with respect to the subject neighborhood, subject property, and the proximity of the subject property to adverse influences in the development of my opinion of market value. I have noted in this appraisal report any adverse conditions (such as, but not limited to, needed repairs, deterioration, the presence of hazardous wastes, toxic substances, adverse environmental conditions, etc.) observed during the inspection of the subject property or that I became aware of during the research involved in performing this appraisal. I have considered these adverse conditions in my analysis of the property value, and have reported on the effect of the conditions on the value and marketability of the subject property.

15. I have not knowingly withheld any significant information from this appraisal report and, to the best of my knowledge, all statements and information in this appraisal report are true and correct.

16. I stated in this appraisal report my own personal, unbiased, and professional analysis, opinions, and conclusions, which are subject only to the assumptions and limiting conditions in this appraisal report.

17. I have no present or prospective interest in the property that is the subject of this report, and I have no present or prospective personal interest or bias with respect to the participants in the transaction. I did not base, either partially or completely, my analysis and/or opinion of market value in this appraisal report on the race, color, religion, sex, age, marital status, handicap, familial status, or national origin of either the prospective owners or occupants of the subject property or of the present owners or occupants of the properties in the vicinity of the subject property or on any other basis prohibited by law.

18. My employment and/or compensation for performing this appraisal or any future or anticipated appraisals was not conditioned on any agreement or understanding, written or otherwise, that I would report (or present analysis supporting) a predetermined specific value, a predetermined minimum value, a range or direction in value, a value that favors the cause of any party, or the attainment of a specific result or occurrence of a specific subsequent event (such as approval of a pending mortgage loan application).

19. I personally prepared all conclusions and opinions about the real estate that were set forth in this appraisal report. If I relied on significant real property appraisal assistance from any individual or individuals in the performance of this appraisal or the preparation of this appraisal report, I have named such individual(s) and disclosed the specific tasks performed in this appraisal report. I certify that any individual so named is qualified to perform the tasks. I have not authorized anyone to make a change to any item in this appraisal report; therefore, any change made to this appraisal is unauthorized and I will take no responsibility for it.

20. I identified the lender/client in this appraisal report who is the individual, organization, or agent for the organization that ordered and will receive this appraisal report.

Individual Condominium Unit Appraisal Report   File # 6153

21. The lender/client may disclose or distribute this appraisal report to: the borrower; another lender at the request of the borrower; the mortgagee or its successors and assigns; mortgage insurers; government sponsored enterprises; other secondary market participants; data collection or reporting services; professional appraisal organizations; any department, agency, or instrumentality of the United States; and any state, the District of Columbia, or other jurisdictions; without having to obtain the appraiser's or supervisory appraiser's (if applicable) consent. Such consent must be obtained before this appraisal report may be disclosed or distributed to any other party (including, but not limited to, the public through advertising, public relations, news, sales, or other media).

22. I am aware that any disclosure or distribution of this appraisal report by me or the lender/client may be subject to certain laws and regulations. Further, I am also subject to the provisions of the Uniform Standards of Professional Appraisal Practice that pertain to disclosure or distribution by me.

23. The borrower, another lender at the request of the borrower, the mortgagee or its successors and assigns, mortgage insurers, government sponsored enterprises, and other secondary market participants may rely on this appraisal report as part of any mortgage finance transaction that involves any one or more of these parties.

24. If this appraisal report was transmitted as an "electronic record" containing my "electronic signature," as those terms are defined in applicable federal and/or state laws (excluding audio and video recordings), or a facsimile transmission of this appraisal report containing a copy or representation of my signature, the appraisal report shall be as effective, enforceable and valid as if a paper version of this appraisal report were delivered containing my original hand written signature.

25. Any intentional or negligent misrepresentation(s) contained in this appraisal report may result in civil liability and/or criminal penalties including, but not limited to, fine or imprisonment or both under the provisions of Title 18, United States Code, Section 1001, et seq., or similar state laws.

SUPERVISORY APPRAISER'S CERTIFICATION: The Supervisory Appraiser certifies and agrees that:

1. I directly supervised the appraiser for this appraisal assignment, have read the appraisal report, and agree with the appraiser's analysis, opinions, statements, conclusions, and the appraiser's certification.

2. I accept full responsibility for the contents of this appraisal report including, but not limited to, the appraiser's analysis, opinions, statements, conclusions, and the appraiser's certification.

3. The appraiser identified in this appraisal report is either a sub-contractor or an employee of the supervisory appraiser (or the appraisal firm), is qualified to perform this appraisal, and is acceptable to perform this appraisal under the applicable state law.

4. This appraisal report complies with the Uniform Standards of Professional Appraisal Practice that were adopted and promulgated by the Appraisal Standards Board of The Appraisal Foundation and that were in place at the time this appraisal report was prepared.

5. If this appraisal report was transmitted as an "electronic record" containing my "electronic signature," as those terms are defined in applicable federal and/or state laws (excluding audio and video recordings), or a facsimile transmission of this appraisal report containing a copy or representation of my signature, the appraisal report shall be as effective, enforceable and valid as if a paper version of this appraisal report were delivered containing my original hand written signature.

APPRAISER	SUPERVISORY APPRAISER (ONLY IF REQUIRED)
Signature _____	Signature _____
Name _____	Name _____
Company Name _____	Company Name _____
Company Address _____	Company Address _____
Telephone Number _____	Telephone Number _____
Email Address _____	Email Address _____
Date of Signature and Report 12/04/2006	Date of Signature _____
Effective Date of Appraisal 12/02/2006	State Certification # _____
State Certification # Residential Appraiser	or State License # _____
or State License # _____	State _____
or Other _____ State # _____	Expiration Date of Certification or License _____
State CO	
Expiration Date of Certification or License 12/31/2006	SUBJECT PROPERTY
	☐ Did not inspect subject property
ADDRESS OF PROPERTY APPRAISED	☐ Did inspect exterior of subject property from street
12506 E Cornell Ave, # 103	Date of Inspection _____
	☐ Did inspect interior and exterior of subject property
APPRAISED VALUE OF SUBJECT PROPERTY $ 107,000	Date of Inspection _____
LENDER/CLIENT	
Name _____	COMPARABLE SALES
Company Name _____	☐ Did not inspect exterior of comparable sales from street
Company Address _____	☐ Did inspect exterior of comparable sales from street
	Date of Inspection _____
Email Address _____	

DEFINITION OF MARKET VALUE: The most probable price which a property should bring in a competitive and open market under all conditions requisite to a fair sale, the buyer and seller, each acting prudently, knowledgeably and assuming the price is not affected by undue stimulus. Implicit in this definition is the consummation of a sale as of a specified date and the passing of title from seller to buyer under conditions whereby: (1) buyer and seller are typically motivated; (2) both parties are well informed or well advised, and each acting in what he considers his own best interest; (3) a reasonable time is allowed for exposure in the open market; (4) payment is made in terms of cash in U.S. dollars or in terms of financial arrangements comparable thereto; and (5) the price represents the normal consideration for the property sold unaffected by special or creative financing or sales concessions* granted by anyone associated with the sale.

* Adjustments to the comparables must be made for special or creative financing or sales concessions. No adjustments are necessary for those costs which are normally paid by sellers as a result of tradition or law in a market area; these costs are readily identifiable since the seller pays these costs in virtually all sales transactions. Special or creative financing adjustments can be made to the comparable property by comparisons to financing terms offered by a third party institutional lender that is not already involved in the property or transaction. Any adjustment should not be calculated on a mechanical dollar for dollar cost of the financing or concession but the dollar amount of any adjustment should approximate the market's reaction to the financing or concessions based on the appraiser's judgement.

STATEMENT OF LIMITING CONDITIONS AND APPRAISER'S CERTIFICATION

CONTINGENT AND LIMITING CONDITIONS: The appraiser's certification that appears in the appraisal report is subject to the following conditions:

1. The appraiser will not be responsible for matters of a legal nature that affect either the property being appraised or the title to it. The appraiser assumes that the title is good and marketable and, therefore, will not render any opinions about the title. The property is appraised on the basis of it being under responsible ownership.

2. The appraiser has provided a sketch in the appraisal report to show approximate dimensions of the improvements and the sketch is included only to assist the reader of the report in visualizing the property and understanding the appraiser's determination of its size.

3. The appraiser has examined the available flood maps that are provided by the Federal Emergency Management Agency (or other data sources) and has noted in the appraisal report whether the subject site is located in an identified Special Flood Hazard Area. Because the appraiser is not a surveyor, he or she makes no guarantees, express or implied, regarding this determination.

4. The appraiser will not give testimony or appear in court because he or she made an appraisal of the property in question, unless specific arrangements to do so have been made beforehand.

5. The appraiser has estimated the value of the land in the cost approach at its highest and best use and the improvements at their contributory value. These separate valuations of the land and improvements must not be used in conjunction with any other appraisal and are invalid if they are so used.

6. The appraiser has noted in the appraisal report any adverse conditions (such as, needed repairs, depreciation, the presence of hazardous wastes, toxic substances, etc.) observed during the inspection of the subject property or that he or she became aware of during the normal research involved in performing the appraisal. Unless otherwise stated in the appraisal report, the appraiser has no knowledge of any hidden or unapparent conditions of the property or adverse environmental conditions (including the presence of hazardous wastes, toxic substances, etc.) that would make the property more or less valuable, and has assumed that there are no such conditions and makes no guarantees or warranties, express or implied, regarding the condition of the property. The appraiser will not be responsible for any such conditions that do exist or for any engineering or testing that might be required to discover whether such conditions exist. Because the appraiser is not an expert in the field of environmental hazards, the appraisal report must not be considered as an environmental assessment of the property.

7. The appraiser obtained the information, estimates, and opinions that were expressed in the appraisal report from sources that he or she considers to be reliable and believes them to be true and correct. The appraiser does not assume responsibility for the accuracy of such items that were furnished by other parties.

8. The appraiser will not disclose the contents of the appraisal report except as provided for in the Uniform Standards of Professional Appraisal Practice.

9. The appraiser has based his or her appraisal report and valuation conclusion for an appraisal that is subject to satisfactory completion, repairs, or alterations on the assumption that completion of the improvements will be performed in a workmanlike manner.

10. The appraiser must provide his or her prior written consent before the lender/client specified in the appraisal report can distribute the appraisal report (including conclusions about the property value, the appraiser's identity and professional designations, and references to any professional appraisal organizations or the firm with which the appraiser is associated) to anyone other than the borrower; the mortgagee or its successors and assigns; the mortgage insurer; consultants; professional appraisal organizations; any state or federally approved financial institution; or any department, agency, or instrumentality of the United States or any state or the District of Columbia; except that the lender/client may distribute the property description section of the report only to data collection or reporting service(s) without having to obtain the appraiser's prior written consent. The appraiser's written consent and approval must also be obtained before the appraisal can be conveyed by anyone to the public through advertising, public relations, news, sales, or other media.

APPRAISER'S CERTIFICATION: The Appraiser certifies and agrees that:

1. I have researched the subject market area and have selected a minimum of three recent sales of properties most similar and proximate to the subject property for consideration in the sales comparison analysis and have made a dollar adjustment when appropriate to reflect the market reaction to those items of significant variation. If a significant item in a comparable property is superior to, or more favorable than, the subject property, I have made a negative adjustment to reduce the adjusted sales price of the comparable and, if a significant item in a comparable property is inferior to, or less favorable than the subject property, I have made a positive adjustment to increase the adjusted sales price of the comparable.

2. I have taken into consideration the factors that have an impact on value in my development of the estimate of market value in the appraisal report. I have not knowingly withheld any significant information from the appraisal report and I believe, to the best of my knowledge, that all statements and information in the appraisal report are true and correct.

3. I stated in the appraisal report only my own personal, unbiased, and professional analysis, opinions, and conclusions, which are subject only to the contingent and limiting conditions specified in this form.

4. I have no present or prospective interest in the property that is the subject to this report, and I have no present or prospective personal interest or bias with respect to the participants in the transaction. I did not base, either partially or completely, my analysis and/or the estimate of market value in the appraisal report on the race, color, religion, sex, handicap, familial status, or national origin of either the prospective owners or occupants of the subject property or of the present owners or occupants of the properties in the vicinity of the subject property.

5. I have no present or contemplated future interest in the subject property, and neither my current or future employment nor my compensation for performing this appraisal is contingent on the appraised value of the property.

6. I was not required to report a predetermined value or direction in value that favors the cause of the client or any related party, the amount of the value estimate, the attainment of a specific result, or the occurrence of a subsequent event in order to receive my compensation and/or employment for performing the appraisal. I did not base the appraisal report on a requested minimum valuation, a specific valuation, or the need to approve a specific mortgage loan.

7. I performed this appraisal in conformity with the Uniform Standards of Professional Appraisal Practice that were adopted and promulgated by the Appraisal Standards Board of The Appraisal Foundation and that were in place as of the effective date of this appraisal, with the exception of the departure provision of those Standards, which does not apply. I acknowledge that an estimate of a reasonable time for exposure in the open market is a condition in the definition of market value and the estimate I developed is consistent with the marketing time noted in the neighborhood section of this report, unless I have otherwise stated in the reconciliation section.

8. I have personally inspected the interior and exterior areas of the subject property and the exterior of all properties listed as comparables in the appraisal report. I further certify that I have noted any apparent or known adverse conditions in the subject improvements, on the subject site, or on any site within the immediate vicinity of the subject property of which I am aware and have made adjustments for these adverse conditions in my analysis of the property value to the extent that I had market evidence to support them. I have also commented about the effect of the adverse conditions on the marketability of the subject property.

9. I personally prepared all conclusions and opinions about the real estate that were set forth in the appraisal report. If I relied on significant professional assistance from any individual or individuals in the performance of the appraisal or the preparation of the appraisal report, I have named such individual(s) and disclosed the specific tasks performed by them in the reconciliation section of this appraisal report. I certify that any individual so named is qualified to perform the tasks. I have not authorized anyone to make a change to any item in the report; therefore, if an unauthorized change is made to the appraisal report, I will take no responsibility for it.

SUPERVISORY APPRAISER'S CERTIFICATION: If a supervisory appraiser signed the appraisal report, he or she certifies and agrees that: I directly supervise the appraiser who prepared the appraisal report, have reviewed the appraisal report, agree with the statements and conclusions of the appraiser, agree to be bound by the appraiser's certifications numbered 4 through 7 above, and am taking full responsibility for the appraisal and the appraisal report.

ADDRESS OF PROPERTY APPRAISED: 12506 E Cornell Ave

APPRAISER:	**SUPERVISORY APPRAISER (only if required):**
Signature: _____	Signature: _____
Name: _____	Name: _____
Date Signed: _____	Date Signed: _____
State Certification #: _____	State Certification #: _____
or State License #: _____	or State License #: _____
State: CO	State: _____
Expiration Date of Certification or License: 12/31/2006	Expiration Date of Certification or License: _____

☐ Did   ☐ Did Not Inspect Property

File No. 6153 Page #13

Subject Photo Page

Borrower/Client				
Property Address				
City	County	State CO		Zip Code
Lender				

Subject Front
12506 E Cornell Ave, # 103
Sales Price
Gross Living Area   1,022
Total Rooms   5
Total Bedrooms   2
Total Bathrooms   2
Location   Spinnaker Run
View   Neighborhood
Site   Typical for area
Quality   Average
Age   26 Yrs

Subject Rear

Subject Street

Comparable Photo Page

Borrower/Client			
Property Address 12506 E Cornell Ave			
City	County	State CO	Zip Code
Lender			

Comparable 1
3012 S. Ursula Circle #302
Prox. to Subject	0.20 miles
Sale Price	109,000
Gross Living Area	1,016
Total Rooms	5
Total Bedrooms	2
Total Bathrooms	2
Location	Spinnaker Run
View	Neighborhood
Site	Typical For Area
Quality	Average
Age	25 Yrs

Comparable 2
3063 S. Ursula Circle #102
Prox. to Subject	0.26 miles
Sale Price	110,000
Gross Living Area	1,016
Total Rooms	5
Total Bedrooms	2
Total Bathrooms	2
Location	Spinnaker Run
View	Neighborhood
Site	Typical For Area
Quality	Average
Age	25 Yrs

Comparable 3
12502 E. Evans Circle #C
Prox. to Subject	0.98 miles
Sale Price	109,900
Gross Living Area	838
Total Rooms	4
Total Bedrooms	1
Total Bathrooms	1
Location	Champagne
View	Neighborhood
Site	Typical for area
Quality	Average
Age	24 Yrs

File No. 6153 Page #17

Location Map

Borrower/Client				
Property Address 12506 E Cornell Ave				
City	County		State CO	Zip Code
Lender				

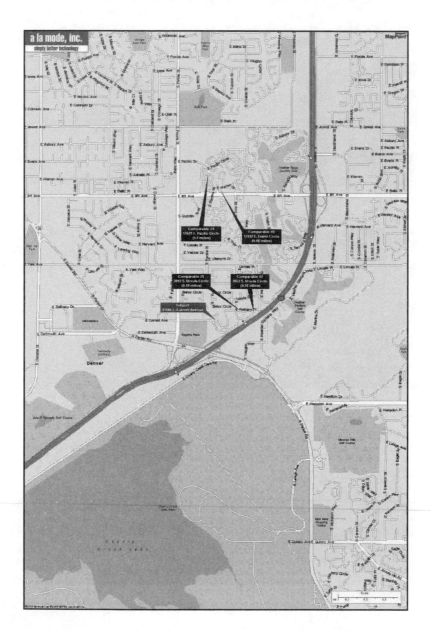

File No. 6153 Page #18

Building Sketch (Page - 1)

Borrower/Client				
Property Address 12506 E Cornell Ave				
City	County		State CO	Zip Code
Lender				

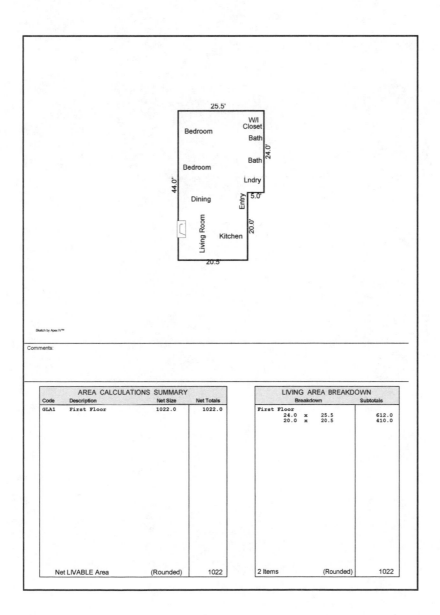

Sketch by Apex IV™

Comments:

AREA CALCULATIONS SUMMARY			
Code	Description	Net Size	Net Totals
GLA1	First Floor	1022.0	1022.0
	Net LIVABLE Area	(Rounded)	1022

LIVING AREA BREAKDOWN		
Breakdown		Subtotals
First Floor		
24.0 x 25.5		612.0
20.0 x 20.5		410.0
2 Items	(Rounded)	1022

INDEX

With products serving children, adults, schools and businesses, Kaplan has an educational solution for every phase of learning.

KIDS AND SCHOOLS

SCORE! Educational Centers offer individualized tutoring programs in reading, math, writing and other subjects for students ages 4-14 at more than 160 locations across the country. We help students achieve their academic potential while developing self-confidence and a love of learning. ***www.escore.com***

We also partner with schools and school districts through Kaplan K12 Learning Services to provide instructional programs that improve results and help all students achieve. We support educators with professional development, innovative technologies, and core and supplemental curriculum to meet state standards. ***www.kaplank12.com***

TEST PREP AND ADMISSIONS

Kaplan Test Prep and Admissions prepares students for more than 80 standardized tests, including entrance exams for secondary school, college and graduate school, as well as English language and professional licensing exams. We also offer private tutoring and one-on-one admissions guidance. ***www.kaptest.com***

HIGHER EDUCATION

Kaplan Higher Education offers postsecondary programs in fields such as business, criminal justice, health care, education, and information technology through more than 70 campuses in the U.S. and abroad, as well as online programs through Kaplan University and Concord Law School. ***www.khec.com*** • ***www.kaplan.edu*** • ***www.concordlawschool.edu***

PROFESSIONAL

If you are looking to start a new career or advance in your field, Kaplan Professional offers training to obtain and maintain professional licenses and designations in the accounting, financial services, real estate and technology industries. We also work with businesses to develop solutions to satisfy regulatory mandates for tracking and compliance. ***www.kaplanprofessional.com***

Kaplan helps individuals achieve their educational and career goals. We build futures one success story at a time.